Cambridge Elements ≡

Elements in Language Teaching
edited by
Heath Rose
Linacre College, University of Oxford
Jim McKinley
University College London

TECHNOLOGY AND LANGUAGE TEACHING

Ursula Stickler
The Open University

CAMBRIDGE
UNIVERSITY PRESS

University Printing House, Cambridge CB2 8BS, United Kingdom

One Liberty Plaza, 20th Floor, New York, NY 10006, USA

477 Williamstown Road, Port Melbourne, VIC 3207, Australia

314–321, 3rd Floor, Plot 3, Splendor Forum, Jasola District Centre,
New Delhi – 110025, India

103 Penang Road, #05–06/07, Visioncrest Commercial, Singapore 238467

Cambridge University Press is part of the University of Cambridge.

It furthers the University's mission by disseminating knowledge in the pursuit of
education, learning, and research at the highest international levels of excellence.

www.cambridge.org
Information on this title: www.cambridge.org/9781108812795
DOI: 10.1017/9781108874403

First published 2022

A catalogue record for this publication is available from the British Library.

ISBN 978-1-108-81279-5 Paperback
ISSN 2632-4415 (online)
ISSN 2632-4407 (print)

Additional resources for this publication at www.cambridge.org/stickler

Technology and Language Teaching

Elements in Language Teaching

DOI: 10.1017/9781108874403
First published online: March 2022

Ursula Stickler
The Open University

Author for correspondence: Ursula Stickler, u.stickler@open.ac.uk

Abstract: *Technology and Language Teaching* is a practical guide for language teachers intending to upgrade their online teaching. During the COVID-19 pandemic many teachers were forced to move their teaching online without proper preparation and support. This has led to frustration and stress, and sometimes decisions based not on sound pedagogy but on technological constraints, requirements, and opportunities. To balance this negative experience, a research-based, pedagogy-focussed approach has been taken in this Element: step by step teachers are shown how to make decisions about the choice and usage of online tools, how to adapt their pedagogy and teaching strategies to fit with online learning environments, and how to create a positive learning experience for their students. In six sections this Element takes teachers from epistemological considerations to learning theories, from teacher-centred to learner-centred online tuition, and from technological needs to pedagogic choice, ending with suggestions on how to future-proof language teaching.

Keywords: online language teaching, professional development, online learning environments, language teaching, research-based pedagogy

ISBNs: 9781108812795 (PB), 9781108874403 (OC)
ISSNs: 2632-4415 (online), 2632-4407 (print)

Contents

1 Introduction

This Element is intended for language teachers, future language teachers, and teacher trainers. Its recommendations for using technology are based on research and the text will refer to research findings frequently. It will also make the claim that research and its theoretical basis are important for language teaching. However, it is mainly concerned with pedagogy and ways to make online teaching successful.

This first section will start with suggestions on how this Element can be used and how it can be useful. I will then talk about the style used here and in the other parts of the Element, and describe some of the purposes of its features, such as tasks and examples. This is followed by an outlook of all chapters. The Introduction will finish with some explanations and definitions. A glossary of terms used in this Element can be found at the end.

1.1 Using This Element

There are different ways to access this Element – different pathways through the material.

It can work as a thorough grounding for teacher trainees and people interested in the foundations of online language learning. This pathway starts with the theoretical approach, with a discussion of various learning theories and how they fit with language learning and with online language teaching. Readers taking this path might want to skip the practical tasks at the end of each section, and quickly skim the more practice-focussed Section 4.

For practitioners concerned with using technology successfully and taking their language teaching online, the pathway focusses on practical and reflective tasks, on different ways of teaching languages and how they can be successfully adapted to fit an online or blended teaching environment. If you are more interested in practical changes, you may want to skip the theoretical Section 2 at first, and maybe come back to it later. You can start with Section 3, which focusses on pedagogy, and make sure that you engage with all the tasks suggested for practical training.

For the very experienced language teacher with a firm grounding in theory and pedagogy, the refresher approach may be most suitable. This starts with recommendations and examples for online teaching and practising the art of online communication in Section 4. Occasionally, when needed, readers taking this pathway can return to theoretical or pedagogic aspects specific to online language teaching.

The Element can also be employed in language teacher training courses using a flipped pedagogy. The main text of the chapters can be set as preparatory reading, the tasks as homework, and the results of the tasks shared in presentations and discussions in class time.

Finally, if you still need to be convinced that online language teaching works, and that it is here to stay, you could start reading the penultimate section with examples from recent research into online language teaching and learning, and how this research confirms success in a teaching environment that may become more of the norm for us all in the future.

1.2 The Style

To justify the different styles in this Element, it is necessary to introduce my own approach to teaching and research. I am a language teacher and teacher trainer, and as such I take a personal approach, trying to create a personal link to my students and to communicate with learners and colleagues in a personal style. In my view, this makes learning more relevant and more fun. As a distance language teacher, I use this style not only in face-to-face communication but also when writing course materials, books, web pages, tasks, and task instructions. Those parts of this Element, where I write as a teacher or trainer, are written in a teaching voice, directly addressing you, the reader.

On the other hand, I am also a researcher, trained in the continental style of written argumentation and the English academic style of clarity and sequencing. When I write about my own or other people's research, I tend to use an impersonal style; trying to present facts and findings succinctly and without recourse to rhetoric or persuasion. For researchers, it is our way of saving time and coming to the point without diversion, and it is more convincing to fellow researchers than a more entertaining or engaging way of writing.

1.3 The Structure

Each section provides a brief introductory overview, dips into theoretical aspects, and refers to research where appropriate. Apart from Section 2, all the chapters also provide examples of online teaching or suggestions for online tasks or strategies. References are provided to allow in-depth follow-up for some of the suggestions.

To deepen your understanding and allow you to experience the principles discussed immediately, every section will contain suggestions for tasks, such as reflections and additional practice. This will make it easier to employ the Element as a workbook or foundation text for a teacher training module; it will also allow independent working through the Element for experienced teachers aiming to upskill. Not all tasks will be suitable for all types of teachers, and sometimes there are alternative suggestions. Where the task, reflection, or additional practice does not suit or is not possible, it can be skipped without losing the thread of the text. If you like the practice-oriented, active learning approach, you can repeat tasks and revisit the notes you have taken on your reflections at a later stage of reading.

1.4 Overview of Sections

This introductory section provides a description of online language learning and teaching, differentiates online from offline teaching, and sketches ways of blending the offline and online elements of language teaching. It also introduces a framework that helps to describe the given teaching situation (STAR).

Section 2 goes to the foundations of our understanding and supports the claim that language teachers need to reflect on their epistemological stance to make the best choices for their online language teaching. It also sketches some learning theories and links our understanding of how humans communicate to the implications of our views on reality and knowledge.

Section 3 focusses on pedagogies and ways to enhance your online teaching by choosing the approach that best fits the given situation. This is grounded in a brief historical overview of the development of language teaching approaches, specifically those concerned with technology-enhanced and online teaching.

Section 4 then points out various options for teachers to shift their practice along three dimensions: the visibility or centrality of technology, the authenticity of communication, and the dominance or the interventions of the teacher. This is illustrated with some examples.

Section 5 shows how we can find out more about how online language teaching works. It provides examples of research projects that prove or disprove our assumptions of online learning. This section also reconfirms how keeping abreast of current research can be beneficial for language teaching, especially in technology-enhanced teaching, an area that changes rapidly and often with unexpected outcomes.

Section 6 provides an outlook into the future of language teaching and prepares us for future challenges. This preparation comes in the form of practical tips for language teachers, and also looks at the future of the entire profession, reconsidering what qualities will make the teaching and learning of languages still desirable in the future, when we will live with technologies that can take over practical functions such as translation or interpreting.

1.5 Online, Technology-Enhanced, or Computer-Assisted?

Nowadays, the word 'technology' is often used to refer to digital tools and technologies in general. This shows how much information and communication technology (ICT) has become a mainstay of our lives. Before starting to talk about the practice or theory of online language teaching, it might therefore be worth considering the delineations of the field covered here. My specialist research area is called CALL (computer-assisted language learning), which was originally defined by the use of a computer, most often in a classroom or computer room. This definition has long been superseded due to a change in technology and technology use. Tools have become less central, and for definitions of a research context, tools are no longer the main consideration. Employing ICT has also become an everyday practice for teachers. Definitions of the teaching context based on either technology or computer use have thus become almost meaningless. Instead, important criteria to describe language teaching practices include:

- **Space**: Is the teaching context purely face-to-face or fully online or is it blended (i.e., part of the teaching takes place in physical proximity and part at a distance)?
- **Time**: Is the communication asynchronous (e.g., email, blog) or synchronous (e.g., Skype, video-conferencing), or a mix of both?
- **Accreditation**: Is the educational setting formal, informal, non-formal, or does learning happen incidentally?
- **Role**: Is the teacher the focus of the classroom or is the learner in the lead?

As a teacher you may feel that you don't have much choice about these STAR (Space, Time, Accreditation, Role) factors. The space and time of your classes are decided by the educational institution, as are assessment and accreditation. There might even be an expectation about the 'proper' role of a teacher, often influenced by national or sector-specific standards. The STAR delineations can help to describe your teaching situation and to identify where it is possible to achieve change or where you are constrained by the given situation.

1.6 Conceptual Not Technical

Throughout this Element, I will continue to refer to CALL as research area. I will also use online learning and online teaching as pedagogical practices. I will try and avoid the term 'virtual' to characterise learning in online environments because the term implies that communication in virtual spaces may have less reality than communication taking place in physical presence. When I talk about online learning, I refer to a context where the majority of teaching and learning takes place online at a distance (i.e., students are not in a classroom where they use tools to go online while at the same time being in the physical presence of other learners and a teacher). Online teaching also implies the deliberate, planned, and pedagogically sound use of online learning environments and tasks. In contrast to this, I would call a face-to-face classroom where some tasks are completed with the occasional use of digital tools, such as tablets or smartphones, a technology-enhanced learning environment.

Blended learning is a deliberate, planned mix of online (distance) and face-to-face teaching and learning. When I use the term here, I am assuming that a considerable part of the teaching takes place online; and – again – that the move is planned and supported with appropriate pedagogy.

The shift from CALL to online learning is not just a question of terminology but a conceptual shift. Online communication takes away some of the aspects of face-to-face communication (just think about sensory impressions, such as smells or the joint realisation of space and distance) and it adds other aspects (e.g., the persistence of digital traces and the option of recordings). Throughout the Element, reasons why online language teaching is different from face-to-face teaching and from teaching other subjects online will be presented. These reasons go beyond the obvious (i.e., the use of technology to facilitate communication between learners and teachers). In short, the online medium changes the way the teacher can help their learners to make meaning of the language they are learning and – as I will argue – this requires a change in pedagogy.

1.7 Task

Reflecting on your needs and your previous experience, choose an appropriate pathway through the Element. To do this, you can either take a rational approach, writing down your goals and aims and matching those to section headings and the description given in the Introduction. Then select the pathway and note down where you will start reading or working through the Element.

You can also take a more imaginative approach to selecting your path by following the dream walk in the text that follows. Some people prefer this kind of mental exercise with closed eyes following a guiding voice, so there is a recorded version of this task available (Sound 1).

Doodle or imagine a path. In your mind start walking along this path, focus on the forward direction it takes you, but also allow impressions from the environment to enter your imagined walk. You can see plants or vistas to the side, hear rustling leaves or a motorway, smell flowers or a deli, and feel the movement of air and the ground under your feet. Keep walking. In the distance you see the

Sound 1 Audio file available at www.cambridge.org/stickler.

end of the path. Allow yourself a pause and think about what you would like to find at the end of this path.

Can you match your desired goal with any of the following descriptions? Then you just follow the recommended path.

a) If you want to find knowledge or understanding, follow the recommended pathway for the theoretical or foundational approach. Keep going and work systematically through the materials, taking notes and following up additional information with outside links.

b) If you want to find confidence and security, focus on the practical pathway, and do as many tasks as you can fit in. Take regular account of your feelings and reflect on ideas and activities. Use others as a sounding board for your progress and be brave in trying out new ideas in the classroom or with friends.

c) If you want to find excitement, adventure, or the unexpected, take an expansion pathway, and add to your already existing expertise by focussing on those aspects that are new to you. Try collaborating with colleagues as often as possible. Give the ideas a chance to develop but don't linger if you think you already know something. You can always come back.

If none of the descriptions fit what you want to find, take an exploratory path and just start by reading in a linear fashion until you decide what the best approach for you will be.

2 Knowledge, Language, and Learning

This section will provide an argument for practitioners to reflect on their epistemological stance. Our teaching is explicitly or implicitly based on theoretical assumptions, and to keep abreast of new developments without following every new fashion, it serves us well to understand the wider context and be selective in the professional development activities we undertake.

I will first talk about connections between knowledge and language, and why language teachers need epistemology for their teaching. I will then go on to very briefly present a small number of learning theories that fit the context of online learning, and finally touch upon the distinctive needs of language teachers, as opposed to teachers of other subjects, in understanding creativity and power relationships in online learning environments to avoid inadvertently 'silencing' our learners.

2.1 Why Language Teachers Need Epistemology

In our everyday lives we take many things for granted: what our senses tell us about the outside world; explanations for experiences we cannot immediately feel, such as gravity; and the possibility of communicating with other humans and, to some degree, even animals. Moving between cultures can rattle some of this 'natural' understanding of the world. Different cultures take different aspects of reality for granted and question others. As language teachers we are familiar with these cultural differences, and part of our skills repertory is the ability to mediate between cultures and thus between divergent views of the world.

Comparing the way that different languages represent the world can help us to understand their underlying worldviews. To illustrate this, I will give a few examples relating to concepts, vocabulary, and grammar.

In Western (Indo-European) languages, we talk about the future lying before us, like a path we can set off on, like a horizon that can be reached. In contrast, Chinese expresses the future using prepositions indicating 'behind'; the future, quite logically in this worldview, is in a space of the world that cannot be seen (it's behind you) and the past stretches before us like a landscape that can be surveyed and catalogued, as its features are set, real, and visible. Other often-quoted examples are how the limits of our language limit what we can think (Wittgenstein, 1974), shape how we think (Sapir-Whorf hypothesis) and even what we can see, depending on the fine-grained vocabulary some languages offer compared to others that are satisfied with just a few expressions. This goes to show that teaching a language cannot be reduced to teaching the translation of words from one form to the other; words transport slivers of different cultures and different worlds. And so does grammar. A language with gendered nouns divides the world into quite distinct categories from a non-gendered language. A three-gendered world 'feels' unlike one with a two-gender division. Also, the way that cases structure a sentence or allow the expression of relationships between concepts can influence how the speaker of this language structures their world.

Diving into a new language, and learning to move between different languages, can thus become a truly transformative experience of learning (Mezirow, 1981). A good language teacher will be able to explain these differences and make them part of this mind-shaping experience. They need to avoid teaching cultural hegemonies (i.e., calling one of these world views the correct or most advanced one, privileging one way of seeing, explaining, or talking about the world, or claiming reality or truth for one structure or description). For a language teacher it is therefore important to be aware of their underlying epistemological beliefs, even more so than for a teacher of other subjects. The following sub-section will look at epistemologies and their impact on learning theories before moving on to those theories of knowledge acquisition that are more suitable to an online environment.

2.2 The Creation of Knowledge

Philosophers have been investigating how we know that which we believe to know about the world for millennia; they also question how reliable that knowledge is. In attempts to make their claim to a certain truth more convincing, they establish rules for knowing, rules for validating truth. One of the results of this constant striving for reliable knowledge is the natural sciences, with their focus on numbers, measuring, and comparing natural phenomena. On the other hand, philosophers also take a keen interest in language, as one of the tools or mediators we use to communicate our understanding of the world to other humans. Language is needed to share our reality and yet language is not neutral. Philosophers have debated how language forms our thoughts (e.g., Whorf, 2012); how it limits what we can talk about (Wittgenstein, 1974); and how it is subject to power manipulation (Heath & Carroll, 1974) as well as being able to exert power over people (e.g., Austin, 1962; Searle, 1969). Without any claim to philosophical depth, here is a short overview of several epistemological stances or beliefs on how knowledge can be achieved. This will become useful when considering how we expect our students to learn a new language and to adjust to a new worldview.

Naïve realism, our everyday stance of taking things for granted outlined in the previous sub-section, is not strictly speaking a philosophical stance, but it serves as a starting point to discuss epistemological questions. It has entered philosophical debates as 'common sense'. That is to say, if all of us were permanently concerned with deliberating how we achieve knowledge, we would not be able to survive. Therefore, simply taking some things for granted in our everyday lives without questioning their truth is good enough for most people most of the time.

Once we start questioning, however, we start looking for something that can provide certainty in an attempt to understand the world or to know the reality around us. Our senses act as our windows to the world and can be used to provide us with 'empirical' information (empiricism); our mind can be used to establish rules and checks that can help to ascertain whether our senses are misleading us (rationalism). However, these approaches to knowledge generation can be flawed. Our senses can adapt to the environment, and thus a person growing up with a tonal language, for example, will hear the distinction between intonation and tonal changes, whereas a speaker with a Western mother tongue might find it difficult to distinguish between them and might need more effort or help. Our mind is not an empty box with a measuring device telling truth from lie. It is constantly formed and re-formed in reaction to experience, learning, and teaching. Considering this adaptability allows us to look at students' mistakes as part of a language-learning journey: it shows how they have formed a new rule and how their thinking develops. The rule may not be correct but it is an indication of taking in new information.

The epistemology of materialism takes the potential flaws of empiricism and rationalism into account and claims that knowledge is derived through a complex interweaving of material conditions (the physical world around us and the shaped environment), historical conditions, and human intervention, such as social and cultural influences. This interweaving is particularly powerful when we consider the digital tools that form part of our students' lives. They are physical entities, and at the same time they are cultural tools in a social environment. As teachers we can use them to influence our students' thinking if we understand how they function in context.

Phenomenology takes a different avenue to avoiding rationalist or empiricist simplicity by introducing the consideration that human beings have a specific condition of being in the world. Through this, we are able to realise that our impressions are not necessarily a truth while we experience and while we think, but that they are our take on the outside and inside worlds – they are phenomena and not facts. Phenomenology or hermeneutics are interpretivist approaches and differentiate between the intellectual endeavours seeking to explain the world (like natural sciences) and those seeking to interpret the world (like humanities, for example): understanding and interpreting use other ways of ascertaining truth than explaining; and methods suitable for the natural environment may not necessarily be effective in the humanities. This may seem far from the everyday classroom experience of language teachers. However, we experience the divergent needs of students asking for simple and clear-cut explanations (e.g., grammar rules) and those longing for an empathic assimilation of the linguaculture (e.g., through art and literature). In a student-centred classroom we cater for both these innate human desires.

Another approach that has influenced our ideas about knowledge is psychoanalysis (Freud, 1900). By taking away the prerogative of the rational mind in human understanding and replacing it with the somewhat elusive concept of the *Unbewusste* (the subconscious mind), psychoanalysts claim that passion, desire, emotion, and drives interfere with our thoughts and actions. Where the conscious mind claimed by rationalist philosophers would allow us to clearly distinguish rational from irrational thoughts or emotions, the human mind as seen by psychoanalysts and their followers interlaces conscious and subconscious, rational and seemingly irrational. Psychoanalysis has influenced philosophical movements such as post-structuralism and provided arguments that place doubt on the existence of a truth altogether. This infusion of desire into language can be exploited by language teachers, not just in the service of increasing motivation but also in the acknowledgement of the power of language to shape our dreams and aspirations.

Regardless of the terminology used and the finer points of argument that distinguish philosophical positions, it is important for language educators to realise how powerful our position is. Firstly, truth and knowledge are fiercely debated and highly desired labels, and secondly, language itself is being used to create, confirm, establish, and defend claims about truth and knowledge, and not always in a transparent fashion.[1] For these reasons language teachers are at the forefront of helping others to make meaning away from their established and ingrained thought processes and patterns. They support learners in moving between not only different languages and cultures but also between different worldviews and epistemologies. The following sub-sections depict, in a bit more detail, a number of contemporary theories that can be used to explain the learning of languages as one form of knowledge creation.

2.3 Creating and Questioning Certainty

This sub-section will outline why a questioning attitude is important for language teaching. Entering a new language/culture/worldview shakes some of our assumptions and beliefs, as described in Section 2.1. This experience can be frightening for some people. Language teachers are experienced mediators between two languages/cultures/worlds and can help to overcome the fear of their learners by encouraging the appreciation of the unfamiliar and the joy of the new.

Creating knowledge or finding the truth are ways that human beings safeguard against the uncertainties of life, the ambiguity of meaning, or the discomfort of misunderstandings. Historically, religion had the role of providing certainty and truth but in the Enlightenment era, rationalism and scientific investigation replaced it. Positivism, the epistemology of natural sciences, and rationalism developed as a response to superstition and the hegemony of religious models explaining the world (for more details, see Stickler & Hampel, 2019). According to positivists, the outside reality can be proven by repeated measuring and comparing, relying on collecting facts and figures. This insistence on objective truth, as opposed to received inspiration or a religious monopoly for truth, has meant that every enquiry critically questions the potential interference from emotions, beliefs, and superstition. While this was a fundamentally revolutionary approach in its origins, rationalism and

---

[1] There are reasons why the words used by post-structuralists and radical feminist philosophers, for example, seem obscure in a framework of positivist epistemological hegemony. However, consider how obscure and even morally corrupt the language of modern physics would have seemed to a nun in the fifteenth century.

positivism have since created their own hegemony (Denzin, 2009), marginalising other ways of describing or understanding the world around us.

As language teachers we understand the difficulties of dealing with ambiguity of meaning. We can see the insecurity caused in adult learners when their vocabulary in the second language is suddenly reduced to that of a child. Because we have to guide our students through this uncertainty and teach them to tolerate ambiguity, we need to be critical of the temptations of any absolute truth, whether this comes in the form of rational, scientific explanations or anti-rationalist inspiration. There are various critical responses to the hegemony of the one truth; the following paragraphs will describe just a few.

Building on materialist philosophies, constructivism has developed as an epistemology explaining how human understanding and knowledge are derived, not from an increasingly closer congruence with the outside world, but by being constructed by a mind that, in turn, is constantly influenced by physical (material), historical, and cultural conditions. In this perspective, no single truth can be found, as the position of the knower in relation to the known is different, not just for every individual but also for the same individual at different times in different places.[2]

Also developed out of materialism, critical theories emphasise the power structures that influence our way of being in the world, often without conscious awareness on the part of those subjected to power. Power is embodied most obviously in political structures, but also, for example, in education, in fashion, in gender relations, and – most pervasively – in language. Combining the forces of critical theory's understanding of power structure and psychoanalysis' scepticism towards the rational mind, post-structuralism and deconstruction establish an ontology (a theory of what is) that undermines all claims for absolute truth, knowledge, authority, or authorship (Derrida, 1972; Deleuze & Guattari, 1987; Irigaray, 1980). Language teaching and learning – as a movement between worldviews – can help to establish a critical, questioning attitude in learners. This democratising tendency can be strengthened by employing ICT and pedagogies suited to online learning.

This short overview of possible epistemologies in the service of language teacher development leads us on to learning theories and their usefulness in language teaching. Although many learning theories are founded on psychological observations and studies rather than on a purely theoretical approach, their basis in different epistemologies is relevant for a deep understanding of

---

[2] Not every constructivist position descends into this radical relativism, as some claim a constancy of structures in the human mind that leads us to develop understanding in a similar way.

teaching: a theory of how we learn needs an underlying understanding of how we know and of what is acceptable and accepted as knowledge.

2.4 How Learning Theories Can Help Online Language Teachers

From the naïve learning theory of the Nuremberg funnel (see Figure 1), the transmission model of knowledge being passed from an expert to a novice, through training approaches like behaviourism, where learning is seen as a getting used to new behaviours, learning theories have come a long way. In the context of this Element only a limited number of theories particularly relevant to online learning will be mentioned: socio-cultural theory, critical constructivism, ecological theory, and connectivism. An overview of different learning theories can be found in Mitchell, Myles & Marsden (2019). An overview of learning theories and their link to technology-enhanced learning can be found in Millwood's very comprehensive HoTEL map (Millwood, 2013).

Socio-cultural learning theory is a collective description of a number of approaches that have in common that they emphasise the social elements of learning. 'SCT [socio-cultural theory] is grounded in a perspective that does not separate the individual from the social and in fact argues that the individual emerges from social interaction' (Lantolf, Thorne & Poehner, 2014: 15). Learning is seen, not as trained behaviour, nor as an accumulation of know-ledge, but as an exchange of experience, helping individuals to adapt to a world where relationships with other humans play an important part. This adaptation

Figure 1 The Nuremberg funnel where knowledge is poured directly into the brain **Source:** Wikimedia Commons: Public domain

is not one-sided: the society or culture the individual adapts to is not a solid, unchangeable entity. Rather, society, culture, and the environment accommodate the individual, and allow them to modify and re-interpret societal norms and cultural expectations (for more information, see Lantolf, 2000; Lantolf, Thorne & Poehner, 2014). The proximity of this learning theory to its materialist roots becomes obvious when we look at how history, culture, and society influence how we learn and are, in turn, influenced by us.

Taking a socio-cultural perspective links research into how learning takes place with pedagogy – the application of systematic interventions to make learning happen. Van Compernolle and Williams (2013: 278) refer to Vygotsky's understanding of this connection as follows: 'as Vygotsky argued throughout his writings, in order to understand the processes of human mental development, we must intervene. In formal, structured educational environments, this entails designing pedagogical programs that create the conditions under which developmental processes may be set in motion and observed.' Underlying this understanding of learning is a relativist epistemology. In other words: what we observe as researchers or teachers is not a reality contaminated by our influence as observers. Rather the opposite: it would not exist unless interference of some form takes place.

Language teachers can use socio-cultural learning theory to evaluate and adapt their teaching tasks to a framework that privileges interaction and negotiation above the certainty of pre-established truth or rules. They will enable learners to interact with others and acknowledge that the culture they mediate is not a fixed entity but always in flux.

Constructivist learning theories can be seen as forms of socio-cultural theory, focussing on the mental processes. In Piaget's socio-cognitive theory (Piaget, 1986), structures of the mind are formed in a genetically pre-determined sequence; the development of children's thinking follows the same patterns regardless of their environment. Whereas in Piaget's theory the content of children's thinking is very much determined by their interaction with their environment, Vygotsky's socio-constructivist learning theory represents the stages of development reached by children as formed in an exchange between the inner workings of the mind and the stimuli received from outside, which have to be internalised before they can be processed (Vygotsky, 1978). Radical constructivism (Glasersfeld, 2007) takes the notion of relativity even further in that mental processes can differ depending on where and in what contexts they are formed, and no reality exists beyond the constructions individuals form in their mind.

For language teachers, the constructivist theory guides them towards emphasising and appreciating their learners' effort in constructing their own rules and mental maps of the target language. Rather than correcting mistakes, language teachers will celebrate them as attempts by the learner at actively participating in knowledge creation.

Critical constructivism (Kincheloe, 2005) combines the epistemological stance of constructivism with the political agenda of critical pedagogy (Freire, 1996; Illich, 1970; Rogers, 1983) to argue for an education that questions the status quo, is sceptical of all forms of privileged truth or knowledge and pleads for a democratic classroom where students and teachers need to work on understanding their position in relation to each other, to the curriculum, and to the wider world.

This approach fits well with a forward-looking professional development for language teachers in online environments where power structures can be defined anew with every new tool developed. Language teachers employing this critical learning theory will make certain that they acknowledge their own privileged position and question the necessity of prescribed standards of accuracy or politeness. As language teachers we may be used to a position of power. Deliberately foregoing this privileged position changes the dynamics in the classroom. This can be achieved by the skilful introduction of digital tools and online platforms that disperse power.

Ecological theories of learning depict similar conditions as socio-cultural theories: the way we think is influenced by the environment we live in; humans adapt, like other animals, and their survival is dependent on successful adaptation. However, rather than privileging human or social influences, ecological theories consider all the elements of the environment. As ecological theories developed from a science approach to human psychology, the underlying ontological assumption (Twining et al., 2017) is one that claims an existing reality, an environment that sends out information stimulating our senses. Our senses, in turn, adapt to the stimuli, process the external information, and pick out what is relevant for the human experience in the given context. A term often used in ecological learning theories is the idea of 'affordances' (Gibson, 1979). An object is perceived by a human in an environment. Rather than simply perceiving (objective) properties of this object, the human interprets the object in the context and imbues it with affordances: what can this object/condition do for me in this context? How can it be useful?

For language teachers in online teaching contexts, the ecological learning theory is a constant reminder that interaction online is not only mediated by language but also by technology. Features of the learning environment have to be interpreted as affordances to allow learners to make the most of it in their language-learning efforts. Tools, online spaces, and information can be exploited in the interest of learning by making the learners aware of their potential, their affordances.

There are similarities in ecological and socio-cultural descriptions of the environment encountered in learning a new or second language (L2), and in the de-emphasising of the individual through the concept of mediation (Wertsch, 2007). Human mediation is not always necessarily present in a language-learning event. Van Compernolle and Williams (2013: 279), for example, claim that 'L2 pedagogy encompasses any form of educational activity designed to promote the internalization of, and control over, the language that learners are studying, whether or not a human mediator (e.g., a teacher) is physically present and overtly teaching'. This becomes particularly relevant when we move towards online language learning.

Building on connectionism (Gasser, 1990), connectivism is a relatively recent addition to learning theories (Siemens, 2004; Siemens & Conole, 2011). Comparing the distributed knowledge present in a large online system – a massive open online course (MOOC), for example – to information processing in neural networks in the brain, connectivism describes how by virtue of being connected, individuals can utilise more information and distribute knowledge across nodes. Connectivism thus de-emphasises the human factor; and tools such as ICT take on an important role. Connectivism is ideally suited for the development of MOOCs and other open online resources as it describes how learning is a process of finding patterns and making connections, thus developing networks and nodes. There is no need for a masterplan or 'master instructor' as learners will create their own connections and networks. As a learning theory, connectivism has its critics. However, whether or not connectivism is a unique learning theory (Downes, 2019; Kop & Hill, 2008) or just an extension of the ecological learning theory is less relevant than keeping in mind the importance of technological mediation in online spaces (Wertsch, 2002).

2.5 Why Online Language Learning Is Different and How

As mentioned in Section 1.6, online language learning is different from face-to-face communication. Regine Hampel argues that technology 'disrupts' (Hampel, 2019); it disrupts the interaction patterns we expect in face-to-face classrooms and the modes of communication; it opens the classroom to the real world. In other words: it changes the learning environment. One of the reasons that this 'disruption' impacts on our language teaching is that many of the signals we rely on when sharing physical space with an interlocutor are missing online. We cannot determine exactly where our interlocutor focusses their eyes (Develotte, Guichon & Vincent, 2010; Li, 2021), we cannot hear all the potentially distracting interferences they have to cope with, we are not always aware when they use additional means to support their comprehension or language production (Satar, 2011). However, rather than claiming that online communication is shallow or lacking depth, we should look at the advantages of online learning, such as the ubiquitous access to resources and opportunities for communication and learning in social spaces. We need to investigate the differences that help us understand the meaning making that takes place online, which in turn will allow us to support online language learners in their efforts.

For example, if we consider time in online language classes, we can either focus on the time lag produced by data transfer across vast spaces, or we can focus on the way that online conferencing platforms often allow parallel communication in different modes (Hampel & Stickler, 2012; Shi & Stickler, 2018). Learners can read a text chat message, listen to spoken interaction and consult an online dictionary – not necessarily all at the same time, but at a time that is convenient for them. Any expectations classroom teachers may have that they can control, or at least survey, all interaction and action going on during the learning event have to be left behind if the learning space is an online platform.

This difference in communication can be seen on a purely practical level as something language teachers have to train for, to practise, and consequently adapt their teaching style. On a deeper level, however, it can also be considered as an epistemological shift: new ways of ensuring that a common understanding is achieved by employing different modes and different checks. To exemplify this, we can look at synchronous verbal online interactions as an attempt to make meaning. A phenomenological perspective would focus on the human experience of what our senses tell us, shaped by our personal history, filtered through our mind. This would normally allow us to empathise with a fellow human being, using a shared language to make meaning together. The online space takes away some of the sensory input normally shared by face-to-face interlocutors; however, there is still our shared basic knowledge, our shared humanity. Taking some of the empathy employed in face-to-face communication for granted might mislead us in online communication, when we assume the person on the other side of the screen might just follow our gaze, experience a similar environment as we do, or is able to project their presence into the online room as they would in a shared physical space. An ecological perspective might try to unravel the impact of the different elements that shape our communication attempt: some of them will be technological, some sensory and human, and some take shape only in the interface between human and technological spheres.

Second-language learning is a special case of online communication in various aspects. Firstly, at least one party of the online communication in a learning event might not be fully able to express their intention in a verbal way; they might also inadvertently express 'foreignness' through a different accent, limited vocabulary, or an unusual choice of structures. This entails an inequality of means – at least of verbal means – of expression. The unequal partner might find non-verbal means to make up for this lack but, again, these means may be different online than in a physical shared space; and in a language-learning situation verbal expression might be privileged, consciously or unconsciously, by the teacher. Teachers need to be aware of this inequality, but also of the fact that for various reasons, the learners might not be able to project all they want to project into their shared online space.

Through their training, language teachers have a number of skills available for coping with these new epistemological requirements. They have a language teacher's trained ability to fill in for missing 'words', be they verbal expressions or other means of communication imperfectly employed. As cultural mediators, language teachers also have a sensitivity for miscommunication and talking at cross-purposes. They have developed a third eye for spotting potential misunderstandings and a number of strategies to counteract them. And finally, they can also bring to the new learning situation the ability to further in their students (as well as in themselves) a make-do attitude and a tolerance of ambiguity, making the best of guesswork and imperfect or incomplete communication attempts.

Traditionally, making meaning would be seen as a uniquely human prerogative but, with the advent of intelligent technology (e.g., artificial intelligence or AI), we have to allow for machines searching for meaning or understanding as well. Connectivism, to a certain extent, looks for this special place of technology in human meaning making, describing the shared space of online human-to-human communication as influenced and shaped by ICT. Does this mean for language teachers that we should give up our expertise in pedagogy and rely on the 'wisdom' of the machine to create learning environments? We will return to this question in Section 6 of this Element, which looks at the future of online and technology-supported language teaching. In the next sub-section, we consider the ways in which understanding the epistemological bases of learning theories can help us shape our own practice and professional development.

2.6 Theories for Online Language Teaching

So how can the learning theory be used to understand and develop online language teaching? Starting with the simple caricature of a naïve transmission model of learning, the online language teacher would be expected to pass on their knowledge of the L2 to their students. This could be done by talking about it, by listing grammar rules and vocabulary in translation, by modelling L2 pronunciation and intonation, and by providing ample input in the L2. In behaviourist models, again simplified, the online teacher would conduct drills for students, forcing them to produce output in repetition and imitating the teacher's pronunciation. As language teachers we know that these methods do not work in the face-to-face classroom, so why would they work better online?

Looking at socio-cultural learning theories, the importance of others in the learning environment immediately becomes clear. This leads to collaboration and group work as important features of the online classroom. Based on this understanding that we learn with others, we can conclude that the content of the communication should be relevant to the individual: no drills about irrelevant grammar examples but real-life statements about personal experiences, performative structures that change what is happening in the real world, empathetic listening, and respect for the interlocutor become central features of this learning and teaching situation.

For critical constructivism, the power issue in the (online language) classroom becomes even more central (Kincheloe, 2005). The teacher, although privileged through competence in the L2, is still part of the group, an interlocutor among others, who may be able to provide scaffolding (see Lantolf, Thorne & Poehner, 2014) where needed but will not abuse their power to select the relevant text and information for each learner. Learners select what they want to present, and their online persona might be quite different from the visible physical person in a classroom. Their world is their own, and only part of this world is shared within the online classroom. In this sense, online learning can be more learner-centred and tailor-made than face-to-face classes and lends itself to a re-consideration of power relationships.

Taking the ecological perspective seriously, teachers need to be aware of the affordances of online learning spaces and make their learners aware of them, as well. This means that teaching often takes place in the form of preparation, familiarising oneself with the space, enabling learners to explore and exploit the affordances of networked and online learning and sharing techno-expertise as well as language competence equally between learners and teachers (Heiser, Stickler & Furnborough, 2013). A similar conclusion can be drawn from connectivism for teachers: making sure that learning can be understood as making necessary connections, finding appropriate resources (including other learners), and realising affordances is a good starting point for a connectivist learning experience.

Language teachers should not ignore epistemological questions but embrace them as part and parcel of their work: as a chance for bringing their unique skills to online communication events and helping to make them successful spaces for shared cognition (O'Rourke & Stickler, 2017).

2.7 Task

A reading list on technology is outdated before it gets into print. Therefore, suggested further literature for this section will take the form of four recommendations on how to stay abreast of current developments in research and pedagogy.

2.7.1 The Systematic Approach

To receive information on new publications in a specific topic area, you can set up an online literature alert. Online search engines (e.g., Google Scholar) or reference management systems (e.g., Mendeley) allow you to set up an email alert. Based on your search criteria or specific keywords, you receive a message as soon as new publications enter the catalogue of your chosen software. Of course, these alert systems are not perfect, and you might get some irrelevant articles. On the other hand, the email alert might just remind you to search for new relevant material.

2.7.2 The Random Approach

If you already have a reading list or a selection of articles you always wanted to read, you can set yourself a time every month to read just one article, and maybe get inspired to dive deeper into the topic. Follow this up by practising what you learned, reading more on the same topic, or discussing it with colleagues. Online conferences and webinars are also a good source for information if you want to move from the random approach to a more systematic one.

2.7.3 The Social Approach

Social media have become an almost indispensable source of information for teachers. Twitter, for example, has a number of online communities of language teachers exchanging and sharing information (e.g., communities identified by the hashtags #MflTwitterati, #LangChat, #ELTchat). These and other hashtags can be searched on Twitter without prior registration. Once you find an expert or a group who deliver reliable and up-to-date information, you may want to follow them on Twitter, and follow up on their recommended reading or announcements of new articles. The advantage of social media is that new research papers are advertised as soon as they are published, and they are pre-filtered so you don't have to search through everything that would appear in a search engine.

2.7.4 The Expert Approach

As a language teacher or researcher you are already knowledgeable and experienced in your particular field. You can give back to the academic community, for example, as a reviewer for journals. Editors often look for volunteer peer reviewers, and you will gain by getting advance access to research. As a language teacher you also bring a very important skill to peer reviewing: you know about giving carefully gauged and supportive feedback and you can balance critique with encouragement. Of course, there is work involved but the overall benefit of reading exciting new developments in your area of interest may outweigh the effort invested.

3 Pedagogy: Fostering Online Language Learning

This section will first look back at the history of educational theories and language-learning theories. It will link these to online teaching, CALL, and the changes continually shaping the contexts in which we teach (the STAR factors mentioned in Section 1.5). It will then go on to explain in detail the three-dimensional framework of technology use in language teaching (visibility of technology, authenticity of communication, and teacher intervention; Shi & Stickler, 2019). Examples of language teaching practice using technology will illustrate the framework and bring it to life by linking it to pedagogical approaches before returning to the relevant underlying theories.

The task for this section is a reflection task and might take you back to when you first started teaching (or learning) a language.

3.1 Histories and Changes

You could be forgiven if you think that educational theories are like fashions – changing ever so often – and that as a teacher you are expected to follow the latest fad. To some extent this is certainly true, and there are or were certain language pedagogies that were fashionable for a short time and vanished quite quickly to be replaced by a new experiment or idea. In any case, language teaching has a history. Educational policies and the wider political context have shaped the language teaching curriculum, for example, in selecting which languages should be learned. There are also changes following the broader developments in educational ideas, learning theories, or expectations of a well-rounded, well-educated person (Pulker, Stickler & Vialleton, 2021).

Some pedagogies have influenced the profession for decades: for example, the change from a knowledge-based concept of language learning (engendering, for example, the grammar-translation method) to a communication-based concept, which is at the root of the communicative approach and has led to task-based (Ellis, 2003) and action-oriented (Piccardo, 2010) pedagogies. A skills-based concept of language use, on the other hand, has engendered teaching methods such as the behaviouristic drill ('and kill') method of frequent repetition, or the audio-lingual method of training the ear and speech organs to get used to the form and feel of a language.

As language learning encapsulates different aspects, such as knowledge about the structures of a language, recognition of its forms, the practice of producing its sounds, the motivation to establish successful communication with its speakers, the need to accomplish a task, and the cultural sensitivity to choose an appropriate way of communicating, this section will not recommend any particular pedagogy but instead map out different practical suggestions for getting students to learn an additional language, and attempt to link these to the technology use that is the best fit to achieve this goal. In starting from the pedagogical aims, we avoid a techno-centric approach that focusses too much on the tool or the medium and is in danger of losing track of the aims of language teaching. As Breffni O'Rourke put it, 'whatever a new technology appears to promise, it does not bring about worthwhile pedagogical innovation in and of itself' (O'Rourke, 2007: 42).

3.2 CALL History

Computer-assisted language teaching and learning (Levy & Hubbard, 2005) is a relatively recent field in language education theories, and yet it has already undergone changes in its pedagogy and boasts a number of historical overviews. From early developments onwards, computers have been used as a means to present and automatically assess language drills such as identification of grammatical forms or gap-fill texts. In more sophisticated programmes, such as language quests, cultural and metalinguistic information is included to provide a rich, pre-designed learning environment for predominantly independent learning. In a later stage, enabled by widely available connectivity, network-based language teaching (Kern, Ware & Warschauer, 2008) uses computers as tools to connect learners with the real world and with each other.

If you are interested in more detailed historical overviews of the development of CALL, you could consult one of the following articles: Bax (2003); Coleman et al. (2010); Jung (2005); Warschauer and Healey (1998). A tool-focussed description of how the use of ever more sophisticated technology changed alongside pedagogical developments at one distance-teaching institution can be found in Hampel and de los Arcos (2013); and a selection of CALL studies, exemplifying how the research approach to CALL has changed over time is available in the article 'TELL us about CALL' (Stickler & Shi, 2016). If you want to keep up to date with the latest technology in the field from a practice point of view, the regular columns of Robert Godwin-Jones in the *Language Learning and Technology* journal are a good base. The COVID-19 crisis and the imposed move to online teaching have inspired numerous articles and collections reporting on good practice or ad-hoc evaluation of changes. Time will tell how many of these articles are concerned with sustainable pedagogic changes or whether some are fleeting impressions engendered by the immediate need of teachers and researchers alike.

3.3 Technology, Communication, or the Teacher?

In Section 1 we looked at a way of describing the given or pre-determined structure of language teaching environments (STAR factors). This section will introduce the axes of change. Technology does influence what happens in a language classroom, and not always in the way the teacher intends or realises. For the development of online language pedagogy, a systematic overview of how different types of technology influence the teaching and learning environment is indispensable. For this purpose, Shi and Stickler (2019) have developed a framework that allows us to categorise examples of language-learning technology in three dimensions or along three axes: the **visibility of technology**, the **authenticity of communication**, and the **directiveness of teacher intervention** (see Figure 2).

The three axes are best visualised as the three dimensions of a cube or three axes that overlap and interact to emphasise how they are interconnected and

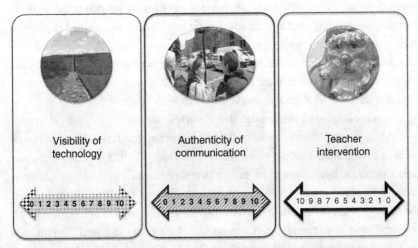

Figure 2 Three axes of technology in language teaching

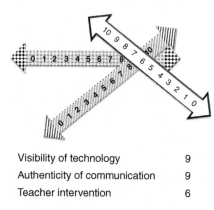

Visibility of technology	9
Authenticity of communication	9
Teacher intervention	6

Figure 3 Interaction of the three axes

mutually dependent (see Figure 3). The axes are developed in more detail in the following paragraphs.

3.3.1 Visibility of Technology

The visibility of technology is described on a scale of 0 (normalised) to 10 (highly visible). Everything, from pen and paper to tablets and smartphones, can be labelled as tools and technology; and the use of a specific technology influences the way we think and communicate (Krämer, 2010). Arguably, newer, less familiar technologies are more visible to us. We notice their use, whereas other technologies, such as counting or the use of pen and paper, become 'normalised', as Stephen Bax called it (Bax, 2011). The visibility of technology as technology thus moves towards zero (0). The same normalisation happens for language-learning apps: when the tool or app is in the foreground, the focus will be on the technology (10), but the more we use it, the less visible it becomes. If a teacher is keen on always introducing new and trendy tools or apps, learners might also focus on the technology rather than the language-learning task. Alternatively, if the choice is left to learners, they might well choose a tool they are familiar with, one they use in their personal life, or one they have found reliable or preferable to the tool the teacher suggests.

3.3.2 Authenticity of Communication

The authenticity of communication is described on a scale of 0 (= inauthentic) to 10 (close to authentic). However, first, a word of warning: authentic language or authentic communication has always been an elusive concept. In the age of networked communication, language itself has changed: language @ internet

(Androutsopoulos, 2011) is different from the written form used in the first half of the twentieth century, and different from spoken language. To place a language-learning event on the authenticity scale, this change needs to be taken into account, rather than measuring online language use against an outdated pre-digital form of the target language.

As mentioned, language learning takes place in a tension between the training of skills and the authentic experience of real-life communication. Training is important, but so is the authenticity of communication. Over time, language didactics have moved from emphasising one end of the scale (training, drills, repetition; 0 = inauthentic) to the other (communication, tasks, action, projects; moving towards 10 = authentic). At the same time content is moving from discrete language items to a holistic view of language, and learner involvement from a rather passive, consuming attitude to active and creative co-construction. Technology can be employed for either purpose. From early drill-and-kill activities, such as gap filling, or Cloze tests, to encouraging interaction with authentic target-language media (Hanna & de Nooy, 2003), activities have been planned to fit the selected pedagogical approach. The communicative approach has brought forward sophisticated scenario-based software, such as web quests (Koenraad, 2006); and task-based and project-based language learning. These methods make use of authentic resources, which are independently researched and employed by the learner(s) to complete a task or project.

3.3.3 Teacher Intervention

Teacher intervention is described on a scale from 0 (very autonomous learning) to 10 (very teacher-centred). In the times of face-to-face language pedagogy, we used to talk about autonomous learning (= zero teacher invention) as something that happened mainly outside the classroom (Holec, 1981). In an online environment the emphasis shifts: learners are working away from the direct control of a teacher and thus have to decide independently when to get in touch and how to follow – or not follow – the directions of a teacher (Fischer, 2007). The weight, depth, and visibility of teacher interventions thus depend not only on the teacher's intention but also on the learner's willingness to follow the guidance. How much planning the online language teacher invests in beforehand to control and direct what language and content their learners will find when searching the web, for example, is a pedagogic decision, as is the choice of how much control the teacher exercises over their learners.

Acknowledging the role of technology and understanding how it impacts on the learning of students gives teachers the option of selecting different tools for different purposes in language education, and shifting the emphasis from more to less visibility of the technology; less to more authenticity of the communication taking place during language learning; and from more to less teacher intervention or, on the flipside, from less to more learner choice and autonomy. Considering these three axes as scales from one extreme to the other rather than inflexible definitions can help describe the different requirements of technology use in language teaching, and empower teachers to take the initiative and shift – if only a little – their use of technology and their teaching practice.

The three axes will be used for the task at the end of this section and for the practical considerations in Section 4. For some examples of where particular tools or teaching practices can be placed, see Section 4.4 and Stickler and Shi (2019).

3.4 Some Examples of Technology-Enhanced Language Teaching Practice

Rather than providing yet another overview of the various pedagogies of online language teaching, I have chosen some illustrative examples of language teaching and learning practice that make use of the ease with which the Internet connects people and grants access to authentic sources of information in many different languages. These types of learning are made possible by the richness of resources easily available on the worldwide web, by the ever more sophisticated use of computer-mediated communication (CMC), and by the ubiquity of mobile and small, hand-held devices and their associated applications.

I will link the following examples, from simple repositories to fully online synchronous tutorials, to the elements of the STAR structure, highlighting where space, time, and teacher role are determined by tool or task choice and where different options are possible. For the moment, I will leave out accreditation and assessment, returning to it later in the section.

A common and widespread use of technology in language teaching is the collection of tasks, activities, and materials in online repositories or inventories. Some of these repositories are freely accessible open educational resources (OERs), some are teacher-created, and others are institutional. One tool-focussed example is the Inventory of the European Centre for Modern Languages (ECML), which collects useful apps and tools specifically recommended and described by language teachers (www.ecml.at/ict-rev).[3] The use of the online space is purely ancillary, as the medium does not impact on the pedagogy of the tasks or materials itself. However, the space can be made interactive by allowing the sharing of and commenting on resources.

---

[3] We will return to the inventory later for the task in Section 4.

Communication is online (Space), asynchronous (Time), and teacher-focussed (Role).

A similar use of online communication is the setting and collecting of homework tasks in an online environment, for example a virtual learning environment (VLE). The pedagogy of tasks does not change; however, the administration of the task is made easier by a systematic overview, by digital tracing and recording. Communication is blended with just some part of the course allocated to online work, asynchronous for this specific use, and it is teacher-focussed as the teacher sets, collects, and evaluates the work.

eTwinning or online classroom partnerships are popular forms of exploiting online communication for language practice. eTwinning is seen as more suitable for younger learners. The twinning is pre-arranged by teachers and takes place on secure and access-limited platforms (e.g., eTwinning Europe: www.face book.com/ETwinningeurope) thus guarding young learners' privacy and online safety. Activities often centre around a topic or are organised in the form of projects (Fearn 2021). eTwinning classes can use a *lingua franca* (often English) to communicate, thus practising a language that might not be a mother tongue to either partner class. The online communication enhances face-to-face teaching, so the use of space is blended; communication is mainly asynchronous during the twinning projects but can contain some synchronous elements. The teacher still has the central role.

eTandem links learners of different languages with speakers of the language they learn online. Switching between the two roles, a learner becomes in turn the expert informant or even an informal teacher of their own first language and thus supports the eTandem partner in their learning. Tandem is chiefly an autonomous form of learning but there is some support through teachers or institutions. eTandem networks provide platforms for linking individual learners or groups of learners and also model tasks for various language combinations and competence levels (Brammerts, 1996; Lewis, 2004). eTandem is fully online (Space), although it is sometimes integrated in face-to-face courses. The communication is synchronous and asynchronous, depending on the tool the learners choose and the skills (speaking or writing) they want to practise. Teachers take the role of language advisors (Stickler, 2001; 2003) and the competent or native speaker eTandem partner often takes on some parts of the teacher role.

An example of fully online language learning is an online lesson or tutorial with video or audio-conferencing software. If it is planned rather than used as a substitute for face-to-face classes, online tuition can change the way learners communicate (Heins et al., 2007; Heiser, Stickler & Furnborough, 2013), enhancing the experience through a combination of digital tools (Hampel &

Stickler, 2012) such as presentation software, online dictionaries, and notice boards. Although space (online) and time (synchronous) are set, it depends on the teachers whether they take centre stage or hand over more responsibility to learners.

After these examples ranging from an ancillary use of online repositories to fully online teaching, the next sub-section will look at pedagogical approaches that can enhance the online teaching of languages.

3.5 Finding a Balance of Power: Choosing a Pedagogic Approach

Certain pedagogical approaches lend themselves more readily to an online environment than others. That is not to say that you cannot adapt a VLE or an online course to whatever pedagogy you favour, but rather that affordances of online learning environments enable new and exciting teaching and learning strategies to come to fruition (Stickler & Hauck, 2006). This section will provide a couple of examples of successful online activities and their underlying pedagogical decisions. An argument for the expansion of pedagogies used in face-to-face language classrooms to include the affordances of the online learning environment will be put forward in the next section.

As mentioned earlier, language learning entails an imbalance of power: the competent speaker of the language possesses the means to express with more ease their intended meaning. Not only will they be able to express more accurately what they mean using varied vocabulary and structures, they will also find pragmatic and rhetorical means for persuading the interlocutor of their argument if they aim to do so. In addition, a competent speaker can employ emotional undertones, giving their speech depth, warmth, ironic distance, or humour with greater accuracy and ease than a learner or novice speaker of the language.[4] This imbalance is in addition to the power difference between teacher, as carrier of knowledge, and learner, as seeker of knowledge.

Online language teaching extends a number of ways to deliberately address this imbalance of power. In the following, I will describe three examples of shifting the balance of power in online learning spaces.

Language teachers do not have to be technology experts. The well-known TPACK model, describing the combination of technological, pedagogic, and content knowledge required of teachers unquestioningly assumes that every teacher will need to acquire technological skill (Tseng et al., 2020). However, when I, together with colleagues, conducted a survey, asking 595 language teachers participating in ICT-related training workshops how they feel in

---

[4] Consider a beginner learner of German attempting to tell a joke in the target language. Not an easy task and often not successful.

situations where their students know more about ICT than them or are more skilful with technology than them, the response was overwhelmingly relaxed: teachers can admit to not knowing everything, they can cope with not being the expert in the room, and are often looking forward to sharing responsibility with their learners (Germain-Rutherford & Ernest, 2015; Hampel, Germain-Rutherford & Stickler, 2014). To quote just one example response:

> 'ICT is a not just 'one' thing to know, it is a vast area of learning. So, as with all subjects, there may be students in your class who know more about one specific thing. Nice! The 'expert' can have a go at trying to share his or her knowledge effectively.'
>
> (ICT-REV workshop questionnaire, anonymous, 2014).

This relaxed attitude and willingness to share responsibility in class might not be true for all teachers in all cultures and learning environments, however, the survey collected responses from teachers across twenty-three countries in Europe teaching languages at educational levels from primary schools to universities.

The pedagogical approach that can be drawn from this finding is: sharing expertise.

To position it in the framework of the three axes, this demonstrates a deliberate move from teacher-centred to student-centred strategies, inviting learners to take responsibility for their own learning and for supporting their peers.

Online language learning offers the advantage of easily arranged authentic communication with competent speakers of the target language. As briefly described in the previous sub-section, language teachers have exploited this affordance from the 1990s onwards, and arranged eTandem learning as a relatively autonomous form of peer-supported language learning (Brammerts, 2003; Cziko, 2004; Lewis, 2020; Little, 2001). By finding learners of different target languages and pairing them online with native or expert speakers who are also language learners, a learning situation is created that facilitates a unique switching of power: A learner of German with English mother tongue, for example, is paired with a competent German speaker who wants to improve their English (O'Rourke, 2007; Stickler, 2004; Stickler & Emke, 2011). With teacher or language advisor guidance (Lewis & Walker, 2003; Stickler, 2003), the two exchange communication online, switching from English to German at agreed intervals. A learner – and less than competent communicator – in one language thus becomes the expert communicator in part of the learning event. Less than a teacher but more than a casual interlocutor, eTandem partners can develop an equilibrium of power, gaining confidence as communicators in their learner role and understanding (or empathy) in their expert role.

The pedagogical approach here is: switching power. The teacher role moves along the axis from expert in the centre to a facilitator, and organiser who prepares the ground but then moves into the background, staying available as advisor when needed. Communication, on the other hand, moves up the scale, to almost fully authentic (8 or 9). The individual exchanges between eTandem partners might well approach full authenticity; however, the setting is still pedagogic and based on the agreement of a peer-learning exchange.

As a third example, I will focus on the ease with which authentic texts and information are available in online language learning. Teachers can prepare materials for the classroom but also send their learners on webquests (Aydin, 2016; Koenraad, 2006) or set them tasks (Ellis, 2003) to find authentic information online. With the help of multilingual websites or machine translation, even the more complex texts become accessible for lower-level learners. In addition to teacher-led tasks or quests, groups of learners can also work more independently. They select a topic or a project (Elam & Nesbitt, 2012) they are interested in, negotiate distribution of tasks, collect information, prepare a presentation in the target language, and share this with the class. In addition to practising receptive language skills in gathering online information, and productive language skills when presenting their project results, learners also gain skills in digital literacy by searching for, selecting, and evaluating information; summarising, citing, and incorporating sources; and communicating online with peers, their teacher, and sometimes also target-language interlocutors. Learners are also encouraged to develop or increase their group and team working skills, their collaboration and their project management skills.

This pedagogic approach, taking advantage of the affordances of the online space, is known as project-based language learning (Sampurna, 2019). In terms of this framework of technology use (Shi & Stickler, 2019), the approach limits teacher intervention considerably (2 or 3), as even the choice of topic is left to students. The authenticity of communication is high in the receptive phase of project work, where students gather information from authentic online sources (7 or 8). However, during the production phase, where lower-level students might feel hesitant to speak or write for an authentic target-language audience, the learning space can potentially be made safe (and thus less authentic) by limiting the online audience to invited peers, other teachers, or sympathetic target-language speakers.

3.6 From Pedagogic Choice to Technology Use

Starting with pedagogy and adding technology as a means to achieve good results chimes with the concept of 'technology-rich environments' as described by Zinger, Tate, and Warschauer (2017). It avoids a techno-centric approach that can often be found when new technologies are introduced in an educational context. To describe it slightly cynically: this techno-centric approach makes the assumption that if you provide enough devices, and upload the latest software, you can just expect teachers to get on with the job of moving their teaching online. The results of such a neglect of proper training and preparation often leave teachers frustrated and learners disappointed, not to mention the waste of resources. There is a need for thorough and tailor-made training of language teachers to choose the right tool for the task and become confident and competent in the use of ICT (Stickler, Hampel & Emke, 2020). The question is not how much teachers need to know but what is useful; not how they will learn new technical skills but whether they need to be experts in all areas and all the time. The fundamental change is one in pedagogy or in teacher role, not one in technology.

As the examples have shown, online spaces lend themselves to letting go of power and making the learning more democratic and mutual. If we take this shift in power relations in online learning and the change of teacher role to support and scaffolding seriously, tasks such as controlling and testing also have to change. Accreditation and assessment will need to be adapted gradually for online language teaching and learning. We need to re-consider what we train our learners for. If it is authentic communication – as is practised online in the twenty-first century – we need to acknowledge the use of online tools, machine translation, and text-to-speech conversion (Henshaw, 2020). Testing comprehension of target-language texts becomes meaningless if learners can just as easily use a tool that quickly translates the text into their native language. Maybe we need to test students' skilful employment of all available tools to make meaning in negotiation with more or less competent speakers of the target language rather than setting tasks that a computer can fulfil quicker and better. In communicating with competent speakers spontaneously online, empathy and tolerance of ambiguity might become more important than accuracy.

Changing our understanding of assessment will take time. It is a reality of formal education that some form of examination and proof needs to be provided to lend credibility to an institution's accreditation. However, we need to work with technology and not against it when we are trying to make our learners fit for a world of online and offline communication in the target language. In a recent project at the Open University, distance teachers and students were asked about the use of machine translation tools and what they consider cheating or plagiarism as opposed to pedagogically valuable practice (Lindeiner-Stráský et al., 2021). All the teachers were familiar with online translation tools and a majority found some pedagogic value in their use in language learning. Students agreed with this and came up with creative ideas and suggestions on how machine translation can be used for language practice, checking their homework, and checking pronunciation of individual words. For assessment, teachers and students had clear ideas how to distinguish between cheating and a legitimate use of online translation tools to support, for example, a writing assignment.

Considering practical changes such as integrating the use of online translation tools into legitimate assessment tasks does not happen in a vacuum. Teachers' and learners' opinions and strategies are based on their beliefs about learning, knowledge, and the nature of reality, or in other words, their epistemological beliefs. In the penultimate sub-section of this section, I will therefore quickly link back to the theoretical considerations of Section 2 before moving on to the practical task.

3.7 Justifying Pedagogical Change

If I want to convince someone of the best way to learn a language, it helps if I can support my beliefs with a link to learning theories more generally. A learning theory explains how a less knowledgeable or less skilful person becomes a knower, an apprentice becomes a master. And pedagogy expresses our ways of making this happen, of supporting or scaffolding these developments. If you want to link this back to epistemologies, you can refer back to Sections 2.2 and 2.3 and consider whether your pedagogic choices rely on a set of hierarchical rules (rationalism), the dominance of the senses (empiricism) or an openness to different interpretations of reality (relativism), linked to material, historical, and cultural influences (materialism), power relations (critical theory), or the forces of our unconscious mind (psychoanalysis).

A constructivist perspective emphasises the learning gain through providing opportunities for experimenting and trial-and-error learning. For language teaching, this means creating a space for safe and un-embarrassing practice. Adult learners, specifically, often feel disempowered and embarrassed when they cannot express their complex thoughts in the target language. As an online language teacher, you can help them express themselves differently, encourage the use of digital means, and adjust the online classroom to playful and creative language use, making the child-like quality of beginners' language fun.

Referring to the ecological perspective, it becomes important to shape the environment for learning, but also to make the users aware of affordances of the available tools that they may not have spotted yet. Making the tools useful and the tasks achievable promises the best results. This pedagogy of exploration and individualisation also means that not every tool will work for everyone. Learners will need to be made familiar with different tools and their use, and – ideally – also allowed choice in the selection of their means of communication.

Any critical perspective will first look for the power distribution in the learning environment. It will also support a questioning and challenging attitude towards power imbalances. Ask yourself: why not let learners be teachers if they think this is the more powerful role? As a teacher it might be difficult but potentially enlightening to sometimes allow yourself to be guided and taught by your learners. Specifically in online teaching, as it often takes place in unfamiliar and new environments, it is important to critically examine tools that 'grab' power, those that are designed for inequality (e.g., video-conferencing software with different user-credentials: host/presenter/participant/guest). You can play with the different power levels and see what happens.

If you are working with a post-structuralist approach, you may wish to question the author-prerogative. Not just in the creation of works of art but also in your learners' outputs, a creative use and re-use, or mash-up, of existing materials can be encouraged. For assessment purposes, however, it is still important at the moment to make clear distinctions between mash-up and plagiarism.

You are now invited to reflect on your own pedagogical beliefs in the following task, before the next section will look at why our language teaching is increasingly moving online, at specific online teaching practices, and some elements of training or self-training.

3.8 Task

What are your own underlying pedagogical beliefs?

1. Can you name a specific pedagogy or teaching method straight away?
2. Or do you pick and choose from different methods to provide the best learning experience for your students?

If you chose category 1 above, consider what elements of your teaching are influenced by the choice of technology or tool and which elements stay the same regardless of medium.

If you chose category 2, continue specifying your pedagogical beliefs a bit more by filling in the grids you can find in Table 1. Consider how much of your pedagogical choices are determined by the STAR setting, and how much you are trying to influence your teaching choices along the three axes of the technology in language teaching framework.

If you still feel uncertain, you can also follow the link to an online survey similar to the one we provide for participants in our ICT-REV teacher training workshops (www.surveymonkey.co.uk/r/TaLTStickler). This online questionnaire contains

Table 1 Grids for pedagogical choices

Predetermined			Open to change		
S: Space (face-to-face, online, blended)			Visibility of technology (10 – 0; high-tech → normalised))		
T: Time (asynchronous, synchronous)			Authenticity of communication (0 – 10; teacher-talk → immersion)		
A: Accreditation (formal, non-formal, informal)			Teacher intervention (10 – 0; instructor-led → autonomous)		
R: Role (teacher centred, learner centred)					

sections about your beliefs with regard to language learning, technology use, and your expectations (Germain-Rutherford & Ernest, 2015).

There are no wrong or right answers to this task. The important outcome is the reflection itself: becoming more aware of what your underlying pedagogical beliefs are and – eventually – linking them clearly to a learning theory and to a suitable online teaching practice.

4 Practicalities of Online Language Teaching

This section will briefly discuss the forces behind moving our teaching increasingly online, the skills needed by an online language teacher and the changes in attitude towards online teaching engendered by the COVID-19 pandemic. It will then go on to suggest a few ways of making your language teaching better suited to online environments, moving it along the axes of the three dimensions discussed in the last section: visibility or dominance of technology, authenticity of communication, and teacher intervention. In doing so, this section will take you to one end of the spectrum of teaching languages with ICT – fully online teaching – and outline the skills needed to be successful in this learning and teaching mode. However, many of the skills, tools, tasks and attitudes can be taken from a fully online mode and integrated into classroom-based, technology-enhanced teaching, making it more future-proof and more suited to the expectations of learners who are now experienced in online learning.

The section will help you to make considered choices. Whether you are forced to move your teaching online temporarily or you choose to integrate more technology into your classroom teaching, anticipating some of the consequences for you and your learners will make decisions about tools and teaching strategies clearer.

The task for this section will invite you to set the boundaries for your online learning spaces and choose tools appropriate for the goals you want to achieve with your students.

4.1 Online Language Teaching and Its Skills

In the twenty-first century, specific emphasis is placed on information and communication technologies and their integration into teaching (e.g., the EU's Digital Competence Framework (2016); Lund et al., 2014). The TALIS report, an OECD generated survey of teachers (2018), investigates how prepared teachers feel to take on this technology task, and the results are not promising: 'Only 56% of teachers across the OECD received training in the use of ICT for teaching as part of their formal education or training, and only 43% of teachers felt well or very well prepared for this element when they completed their initial education or training.' (OECD, 2018: 29)

Language teachers nowadays are not only encouraged but often required by governmental guidelines to integrate technology (e.g., Hu & McGrath, 2011), and tacitly expected to be a role model of technology use. Integrating ICT into language teaching does not just mean using a computer to support traditional teaching techniques but to change teaching according to the affordances of ICT and the requirements of a knowledge society.

The skills needed to integrate ICT meaningfully into a language class are developed over time and with support. Practice makes perfect, and practice also gives confidence. In a 2017 eye-tracking study, together with colleagues (Shi, Stickler & Lloyd, 2017), we have shown how much of a difference familiarity and experience make. We worked with one very experienced online language teacher and one teacher who had years of classroom teaching experience but no experience of online teaching. Comparing their online behaviours and reflections we found that the novice online teacher regarded the environment in a *deficiency perspective*, focussing on what is lacking and what she would have done if she were teaching in a face-to-face environment. In contrast, the experienced online teacher took a *difference perspective*, empathising with her students' different experience in an online class and using tools and strategies appropriate to the medium.

Together with the lack of experience and the overwhelming concern with technological deficiencies comes a lack of confidence: even the most experienced and skilled face-to-face teacher can get insecure when working in a new environment. This matches with the skills pyramid developed by Regine Hampel and myself (Hampel & Stickler, 2005) that describes how different skills of online teaching build on each other and the more skilful the online teacher becomes, the better they can focus on creativity and on developing their own style. In the 2015 update of our pyramid (Stickler & Hampel, 2015), we added the new dimension of negotiating online learning spaces. In a time when Internet use and online communication have become commonplace, it is of increased importance to delineate a space that is dedicated to learning and to distinguish it from private communication. This new skill has also come in useful in the experience of a pandemic that forced thousands of language teachers to take their work home and their classrooms online.

4.2 Change in the Face of a Pandemic

If you were working as a teacher in 2020 and 2021, did you find yourself working more with technology than you ever expected to have to do? You were certainly not alone. In a 2010 study, Ertmer and Ottenbreit-Leftwich investigated the conditions for teachers to integrate technology; what makes them change their practice? What helps them to become confident and successful users of ICT? The one thing the authors could not have envisaged in 2010 is that a global event would force teachers out of the classrooms and into online spaces. Many of them took up the challenges with initial trepidation but also with great success. Going back to school for them did not always mean going back to the same way of teaching languages as before the pandemic.

During the COVID-19 crisis and the resulting restrictions on face-to-face schooling, many language teachers had to take their teaching fully online yet did not receive adequate support or training (Ernest & Heiser, in press; Lindeiner-Strásky, Pulker & Vialleton, in press). As part of a team of experts, supported by the ECML, I offered webinars to language teachers across Europe affected by this unexpected move. The webinars took place in May 2020, at a time when many teachers were still struggling to come to terms with online digital tools and distance teaching. We offered the training in three languages (English, French, and German), and based the content on our ICT-REV workshops. More than 2,800 took up the offer and enrolled in the webinars. To provide useful responses to the needs of the participants and to help us tailor the webinars, we asked participants to fill in a short questionnaire before the live training sessions. In one of the questions we asked what elements of the – imposed – online teaching they would like to take back to their classrooms once 'normal' teaching would resume.

Before I report some of the results, consider for yourself, what your response would have been. Have you been forced to use unexpected, unfamiliar tools or methods once? Did you get to like some of the elements? Did you succeed in adapting your previous methods to the new situation?

We received 2,386 responses to our questionnaire, with 2,249 teachers answering the question 'Which aspect(s) of your current online experience will you take back into your 'regular' teaching?' I manually scanned and coded the – mostly short – responses in the original language, using machine translation tools to augment my limited knowledge of French when necessary. Apart from five disenfranchised teachers who would prefer to take 'nothing' back to their familiar face-to-face environment, there was a considerable number of teachers who evidently started thinking differently about teaching. Of course, quite a few responses reflect the uncertainty of the times; twenty-one saying they don't know (yet) what they will take back, partly because they had not used any online teaching ('THE ONLY THING I DO WITH MY STUDENTS IS TO SEND THEM ACTIVITIES BY E-MAIL'). Many teachers mentioned specific material types, such as videos or flashcards. Frequently they considered introducing specific tools into their teaching, for example, making use of quizzing tools such as Kahoot, or sharing spaces such as Padlet or Slideshare. One of the questions asked teachers to select their favourite from a list of thirty-two tool types described along the lines of tools categorised in our online inventory. The most frequently selected tool types across all three languages were quiz makers and games apps.

When considering what they wish to retain in their future practice, some teachers think only of the practicalities of a digital way of working. They describe the benefits of online working as follows:

> No more photocopies. Homework will be assigned there. [i.e., online]

> The use of web 2.0 tools and the habit of storing teaching material on a digital teaching platform.

There is also a realisation of how digital communication impacts on pedagogy and the teacher's role. Teachers comment on the change in their own way of working by describing it as '1 to 1 pedagogy', or by describing their change in attitude:

> Accepting that I don't always know, to which extent each child has learnt a specific content, but trusting that they all advance at their level.

As mentioned earlier, going back to a teaching practice that was common 'before the pandemic' does not seem to be an option for many teachers. The responses show a willingness to change beyond the immediate, enforced move to online teaching:

> I will certainly continue using Web tools, because once the students familiar-ise themselves with them, you cannot go back into 'traditional' teaching.

> I am thinking of taking everything back into my regular teaching and starting a new e- + regural [regular] teaching.

As you can see from this brief summary of just some of the responses, change happened on different levels: On a surface level, teachers realised that they need new tools or techniques to teach online. On a deeper level, they also reflect that, together with these tools, they need the necessary skills to employ them for language teaching. Responding to the question – 'What is the main difficulty you are finding in having to teach fully online?' – one teacher wrote: 'not having the skills needed'.

More sustainable change is indicated in responses where teachers realise that the pedagogies they employ in a face-to-face context do not necessarily work online. Particularly where teachers focus on control and correction, the online environment fails them. Resulting from this perceived deficiency, teachers may experience frustration ('It was not a good experience'); some believe that they have not yet found the right tool, or that the tools are not developed for their type of teaching ('Quizlets, voice recordings ... Not sure ...').

The realisation that there is a difference between being a successful and confident blog author and using a blog as a means to encourage students to stay involved outside the (physical) classroom, or the difference between setting an online crossword and using this tool to reinforce vocabulary for beginner learners, is going into a deeper level of change. Recognising the importance of this pedagogic dimension goes beyond the willingness to take part in an online webinar for skills training; it shows engagement with a change in the way we will teach in the future. This engaged attitude can be identified in some of the responses:

> Ich werde meine Unterrichtsweise ganz ändern. Alle neue Elemente die ich gelernt und benutzt habe, werde ich in der regulären Klasse einsetzen. Ebenfalls werde ich mich nicht davor schäuen, bei einem europäischen Programm mit der Schule oder mit der Klasse teilzunehmen. Wortwolken und Mentimeter werde ich sicher einsetzen. Ich hoffe, von diesem Webinar neue interessante Sachen zu lernen.

> I will change my way of teaching completely. I will use all the new elements I have learned and used in my regular classroom. I will also not be afraid to participate in a European programme with the school or with my class. Wordclouds and Mentimeter will certainly be used. I am hoping to learn new interesting things from this webinar.

By the way: this German quote was translated with the help of the online machine translation tool DeepL (www.deepl.com/translator (free version)) – more about that later in Section 6.

Where true change happens, teachers actually realise the benefits of the online teaching methods, and with varying degrees of enthusiasm plan to integrate these benefits into face-to-face situations. There is a recognition of

Figure 4 Image of a Mexican pyramid (source: Pixabay free online images, URL: https://pixabay.com/de/photos/chichen-itza-yucatan-pyramiden-maya-683198/)

the change in power relationships between teachers and students in some forward-looking responses: More democratic teaching ('Enseignement plus democratique') or flipped classrooms are mentioned several times. The student moves to the centre ('L'élève sera en centre de l' éducation') and is given more power and autonomy ('Asking the students to participate more during the lesson and learning from them how to share things by listening more to what they have to say. Learner independence and learner autonomy to a new level').

4.3 Training the Online Language Teacher and Their Skills

One webinar, one questionnaire, even one week of training cannot bring about the numerous skills needed for online language teaching (Comas-Quinn, 2011; Lewis, 2006), and, as we have seen: confidence comes with experience. In a later sub-section we will look at how moving your teaching online gradually can help develop this confidence. In contrast, comparing your skills to someone else's can lead to frustration or even loss of confidence for some people. If you want to use a tool for self-evaluation that specifically does not ask you to look at other teachers around you, you can consult the established model of the pyramid of online teaching skills (Hampel & Stickler, 2005; Stickler & Hampel, 2015). Particularly if you are engaged in self-training or autonomous professional development, looking at the levels of the pyramid to check what particular skill you want to work on can help keep your training manageable.

Table 2 The online language teaching skills levels

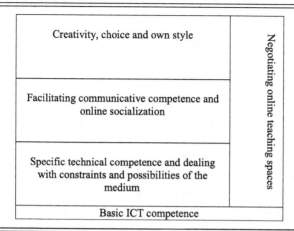

Just to summarise the different skills levels from our pyramids: purely technical skills and being able to use the tools for online teaching are on a lower level of the pyramid. Encouraging communication and socialisation online – an important aspect of language learning and use – are on a higher level and work better if the confidence to master technical skills has already been achieved. The highest levels, creativity and teaching style, require familiarity with a variety of tools that can enhance and encourage creativity as well as reflective awareness of one's preferred teaching style and how this can be adapted to an online environment. Even though reaching confidence and competence in online language teaching might take some time, there is training available to help along the steps, and the task of this section will bring some suggestions of how to move towards this stage without having to completely change your teaching style.

A team of experts from the Open Universities of the UK and Catalonia, together with experts from Germany, Croatia, and Canada have developed a participant-focussed, 'bottom-up' training model for language teachers (Stickler, Hampel & Emke, 2020) based on the pyramid model of developing online teaching skills. Since 2008, this training scheme has been offered through the ECML in workshops across Europe. The ECML as a subsidiary of the Council of Europe has been set up to maintain the diversity of languages across Europe and their teaching in schools and beyond. To date, over 1,500 teachers have been trained in these workshops that take into account that not every teacher will be technophile, confident, or even convinced of the usefulness of ICT in the language classroom. In contrast to a forced move to online teaching, either engendered by lockdown or by governmental top-down requirements, this model encourages the integration of ICT into classroom teaching at whatever level participants are comfortable with. Similar to the task in Section 3, where you were encouraged to reflect on your own pedagogical beliefs, we start the planning of every workshop by enquiring about the pedagogic position of participants (Germain-Rutherford & Ernest, 2015). This helps the facilitators to tailor a training event to the needs of each participant. As Ertmer and Ottenbreit-Leftwich (2010) suggest, aligning teachers' 'experiences with existing pedagogical beliefs and knowledge' and giving them the opportunity to experiment with ICT, take risks, and experience change will help them to integrate new technologies into their practice (Ertmer & Ottenbreit-Leftwich, 2010: 276).

In addition, as part of the ECML's support for online language teaching, an inventory of free online tools and OERs was created by our team. This is very much in line with teachers' requirements as stated, for example, by one of our respondents to the webinar questionnaire:

> Teachers need to have a variety of tools to transform the old-fashioned exercises to interactive ones. Unfortunately all these tools are not given for free. Would you please give us some information about this problem? (Questionnaire respondent, anonymous).

For the online inventory, we collected recommendations from experienced teachers, evaluated and checked the recommended tools, found short user guides, and enhanced some of them with sample activities. This inventory of online tools specifically suited to language teaching can be found on the ECML website (www.ecml.at/ict-rev). It is regularly checked and updated with the help of users, language teachers, and researchers.

Other training resources for online language teachers have been created by colleagues at the Open University (Lindeiner-Stráský et al., in press) as part of OpenLearn resources; and at the University of Ottawa, Canada (Goodier et al., 2021). This freely available resource (LINCDIRE: https://lite.lincdireproject.org/) is specifically focussed on multilingualism and action-oriented learning.

As outlined in the previous section, technology integration comes in stages and degrees: from fully classroom-based language teaching with the occasional use of online elements, such as website content or a specific communication tool for a specific task, through frequent use of ICT for all learner tasks, to blended learning and flipped classrooms where the emphasis is on online- or digitally-based preparation and the classroom is used only for practice and clarifications, to a full online course or fully online independent language learning. The next sub-section will suggest ways of how change can happen gradually by shifting teaching practice incrementally, using the available resources, underlined by a firm grasp of theoretical principles.

4.4 Moving Gradually: Dimensions and Examples

The framework in Section 3.3 described online or technology-enhanced learning situations along three dimensions: visibility of technology, authenticity of communication, and teacher intervention. Technology can be normalised (Bax, 2011) or almost invisible (0 or very low on the scale of 0 to 10), or it can be highly dominant (10) when new and unfamiliar gadgets or apps are being introduced. Communication situations that can be placed on a continuum from inauthentic drill and kill practice (0) to the highest level of unstructured and free conversation with competent speakers (10). Teacher intervention can vary from tightly structured and teacher-led activities (10) to planned and scaffolded but greatly independent tasks or projects (0). Teachers can choose to move their practice along any of these three dimensions. A little change in one dimension might make a great impact on the learning experience of students, and teachers don't have to feel obliged to change their entire practice. Figure 5 is intended to show this flexibility: sliding up or down one scale changes the balance of the overall structure.

To illustrate the impact of moving teaching along these three dimensions, we can look at the eight corner points of the cube, when the dimensions are moved to the extreme point, from 0 to 10 or 10 to 0. To clarify, examples for each corner point are given very briefly in Table 3. Note that the extreme points (10/10/10 and 0/0/0) are purely hypothetical and do not appear in language teaching practice.

In the following, three corner points are used to describe in detail how examples of language-learning activities can be categorised and how teaching

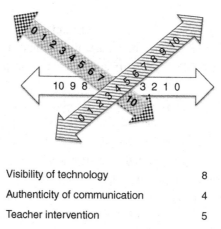

Visibility of technology	8
Authenticity of communication	4
Teacher intervention	5

Figure 5 Three axes of technology use in language teaching

Table 3 Eight corner points of the cube depicting technology use in language teaching

Visibility of technology	Authenticity of communication	Teacher intervention	Example:
10	10	10	Hypothetical and not realistic
10	0	10	In-class pronunciation drill (e.g., NewPepper tone recognition software)
10	0	0	Supplementary online grammar drills (e.g., https://german.net/exercises)
10	10	0	Encourage use of Google Translate
0	10	10	eTwinning under teacher guidance
0	10	0	eTandem with normalised tool (e.g., Skype)
0	0	10	In-class Cloze test with word document or pen and paper
0	0	0	Not a teaching or learning event

can be moved along the axes to change the dynamics of the online or blended classroom. At one extreme corner point, teaching is highly controlled, technology is dominant and highly visible (10), and the communication is not authentic (0). The main reasons for the learner to take part in the task would be the teacher's guidance, explicitly in instructing the student and implicitly in choosing the tool. This highly inauthentic communication would not be found in any normal, real-life conversation. One example for this type of language-learning activity is the use of speech recognition to practise pronunciation or tones. NewPepper, a software application for learning Mandarin Chinese tones, records and measures learner-produced utterances and compares them to idealised tonal productions by native speakers. Transforming the tone into a graph, the learner can compare their utterance with the ideal curve of the Mandarin tones (Kan, 2013). Similar speech-recognition software has been used for other languages for decades (Godwin-Jones, 2009). As the use of this type of software is not common in everyday life, the technology is not normalised and becomes highly visible in the learning context.

At another extreme point the teacher gives up almost all control of the learning environment (0), technology is being used as in the everyday life of students outside the classroom (0), and we find an almost or entirely authentic communication with target-language speakers (10). The teacher does not play a noticeable role in the actual communication event, although scaffolding, support, and guidance has prepared the field for the student to actively engage in learning. The difference between a natural conversation and the learning event described here lies in the negotiation of learning spaces, the agreement between conversation partners that the activity is used for language learning. An example would be a well-developed and well-advanced eTandem learning event (e.g., Batadiére & Jeanneau, 2020) where both partners continue to work independently after the initially scaffolded introduction and getting-to-know phase of their pair work. Another example of this highly unstructured but authentic learning event is the vocabulary learning that players of massive multiplayer online role-playing games experience (Bytheway, 2015).

Considering the third extreme point, low technology (0) and low authenticity (0) with high teacher dominance (10), a classical example would be the use of Cloze tests, written texts with gaps in specific places. Students' reading ability and language proficiency is determined depending on how well they manage to fill the gaps in the text. Although these tests have little authentic or communicative meaning, they are still used in language classrooms for other purposes. The technology used can be really simple, for example, pen and paper (0) or word documents (1 or 2) and thus becomes almost invisible.

After providing these illustrative examples of points on the three-dimensional scale, we will now look at moving along the scale lines in different directions and gradually making language teaching more fit for online teaching.

Taking the dimension of teacher intervention, a language teacher can deliberately move their teaching from one end of the continuum (high teacher dominance, 10) to the other (low teacher intervention, 0) in different ways. One way is to change the task, for example from a multiple choice quiz to an open text question with a model answer. As well as minimising teacher influence and control, it also gives students more power in evaluating their own learning. To be beneficial for learning, it would require learners to be trained in comparing their response with a model. Another way of shifting the teacher's role from the centre to the periphery is to change the classroom dynamics by encouraging peer correction or even peer evaluation in online systems that allow for anonymised feedback (e.g., Peerworks in Moodle). A teacher can also change the pedagogy and choose, for example, flipped learning; thus, encouraging students to guide each other through finding grammatical explanations (Lindeiner-Stráský et al., 2020). This moves the focus away from teacher-led instruction in class time. A change of tool can also impact on the centrality of the teacher. For example, considering the power distribution in a video-conferencing tool by giving all participants moderator rights is a quick method of changing the dynamics in the online classroom. These examples show how a deliberate choice on one dimension (e.g., a change of technology, pedagogy, or task) has an influence on the other aspects and can lead to a change in the teacher role in online learning.

Considering the dimension of visibility of technology from dominant (10) to normalised (0), there are, again, a number of decisions a teacher can take when planning ICT use. Reducing the dominance of technology can be achieved by not choosing the latest and most advanced tool but instead basing a selection on fit and familiarity. Deliberately toning down the visibility of technology through integrating everyday tools, such as Skype, Instagram, or WhatsApp, can help. Another strategy is moving the training for technology use outside of the language classroom (Heiser, Stickler & Furnborough, 2013) and asking students to familiarise themselves with a specific tool beforehand to avoid an overt focus on technology during class time. Similarly, but more radical, is giving students a choice in selecting the tool or platform used for their own learning. Students might well choose those tools they are most familiar with from their personal life, thus keeping the technology threshold low for their personal learning. The choice of device can also support this de-emphasising of technology. If learners are allowed to use their mobile phones during class time, for example to answer quiz questions on Kahoot, the technology will be much less dominant than requiring learners to move to a dedicated computer room.

This dimension also shows how teacher attitude and preparedness to share power with learners influences a move on a continuum from dominant to normalised technology use. For some teachers these suggestions might seem too radical. They may want to keep control of platforms used during classroom time and only allow free choice for homework or personal learning. Leaving choice completely to learners also means that teachers will need to consider the 'cultures of use' (Thorne, 2003). Shifting the use of tools and platforms normally employed for private communication (e.g., Facebook) to a teaching and learning instrument makes a delineation between private use and learning use of a tool or app necessary. One of the skills of an online language teacher is selecting, negotiating, and defining the learning space (Stickler & Hampel, 2015). Teachers need to make it clear to students what the purpose of the tool use is and reassure them that they will not interfere in their private communications. A clear distinction is beneficial, not only for pedagogic reasons but also in the aid of student and teacher well-being.

The third dimension of the technology and language teaching framework (Shi and Stickler, 2019) concerns the authenticity of communication. For language teachers it is common practice to adapt and simplify authentic texts for lower-level learners, thus providing the necessary scaffolding according to the needs of the learners. The abundance of resources available to teachers online means that some teachers and teacher trainers believe that the future of language learning might well be a virtual immersion with multiple and multimodal input that allows learners to 'soak up' the target language (Germain-Rutherford et al., 2021, Godwin-Jones, 2019). But even so, for beginners and low-level learners at least, the teacher will need to select, filter, and prepare materials to make them comprehensible and transform them into a manageable learning resource. Along this continuum, teachers will therefore choose more or less authenticity and more or less natural communication according to the needs of their learners.

Even from a relatively low level of language competence, careful scaffolding can allow the use of online resources that were not specifically designed for language learning. Students can be encouraged to find their own learning resources and exploit them with the help of tools such as speech to text (Blabberize) or machine translation (DeepL). Creating collaborative spaces for project work in the target language through eTwinning or online classroom partnerships (Fearn, 2021) also introduces the concept of authentic, meaningful communication early in a language learner's career. The penultimate sub-section of Section 4 will critically reflect on the usefulness of a framework in different contexts.

4.5 The Epistemological Implications of Dimensions

Consider for yourself how the use of a framework in the previous sub-section made you feel. Do you like the structured approach? Or do you feel doubt and concern? Maybe you are confused or annoyed. This might have to do with your epistemological stance and whether a structured approach matches it or not.

Under certain epistemologies, frameworks are considered indispensable for knowledge generation. Particularly rationalist worldviews prefer an ordered and structured approach that can be shared between different researchers, across cultures and languages, without losing the power to convince. In other epistemologies, particularly constructivist or post-positivist ones, frameworks are considered more like scaffolds or crutches that are used to allow the mind to order and observe events and describe them without the need for excruciating repetition. Placing 'visibility of technology' on a scale from zero (the entirely normalised) to ten (the highly obvious), for example, allows the description of a tool or task as a variable on this scale, and creates a shortcut avoiding the in-detail description of the effect of using this specific tool in the specific learning environment on the individual learner or teacher. Of course, the 'crutch' is not neutral, and every framework potentially limits the view and excludes or disguises important aspects.

It is also worth repeating that the scale is not a judgement or evaluation but purely descriptive. Zero is not necessarily better than ten, and almost all the points in the cube have some value for language teaching and can lead to learning. The framework used here is presented with a word of caution and only used to help teachers place their pedagogic intentions in context. It encourages you to reflect on your pedagogy and your pedagogical aims and supports you in moving gradually from teacher-centred to student-led, from technology-focussed to technology-normalised or from scripted to authentic communication in your language classroom IF you wish to do so.

Reflecting on tool choice and technology dominance also highlights the implications your choices have on the learner experience and how the different dimensions of language teaching conjoin and influence each other. Referring back to the STAR-scheme introduced in Section 1 (Space, Time, Accreditation, Role), the settings of your teaching and the specific requirements of your learners will influence and limit the choices you make. To practise some of the skills needed to establish successful online language teaching, the task in this section will take you straight online, first in your imagination and then to a real online site that can help you choose appropriate tools for your classes.

4.6 Task

4.6.1 Part 1

Starting with the encompassing skill for online teaching, the first part of this task asks you to establish the boundaries of an online learning space.

In your imagination, design an online environment that is inviting, non-threatening, conducive to communication in the second language, and full of L2 input and opportunities for L2 output. You can do this by taking notes, drawing on a piece of paper, or by creating a poster wall with a tool such as Padlet (https://padlet.com/) online.

> I will only answer learning-related queries between
> 4pm and 6pm on weekdays.

Figure 6 Example of an online label: teacher

> Teachers: Please do not read my texts in the
> section "poems and dreams".

Figure 7 Example of an online label: student

Now imagine this environment taking over part of your private communication online. You don't want that to happen, so place no-go signs clearly at the boundaries between the learning space and your own private space.

For example, you could post on your Facebook wall: 'I will only answer learning-related queries between 4 p.m. and 6 p.m. on weekdays.'

Switch perspectives, and do the same from the point of view of a learner: where would you allow your teacher to go? Where is the no-go area of your private thoughts and communication?

For example, you could envisage your students wanting to keep their poetry private.

Making these boundaries explicit and clear to learners and teachers helps in establishing an online learning environment and managing expectations. Find a wording for the no-go sign in the target language that is neither offensive nor unclear. And this is the first part of your task done.

4.6.2 Part 2

Choosing the right tool for a task can be daunting, particularly in the fast-moving world of ICT. There are many good tools and apps around that can help a language teacher. To sort through them, and save you time in selecting, the ICT-REV inventory of tools for online language teaching (www.ecml.at/ict-rev) has pre-selected freely available tools and vetted them against pedagogic criteria.

Think of a language skill that you would want your class to practise (e.g., writing or vocabulary). Then look at the principal functions listed in the inventory and select one that is appropriate for your teaching. Consider whether you want to invest the time in creating your own content or if you prefer ready-made materials. Select tools on the inventory. Look at two or three tools' descriptions for no longer than five minutes each. Can you make a decision already? If not, go into depth for one tool by following up its weblinks. Check out the brief how-to guide or look for comments from other teachers.

Once you've selected the tool, re-consider: does using this tool add anything to the pedagogic value of the task or is it just a gimmick? Would the task work better without technology? Or does the use of technology play a transformative role? Does the tool maybe even allow us to carry out new and innovative activities? If you think the ICT-element is a benefit or if you want to future-proof your teaching, go ahead and adapt or create your task using the tool.

Once you've tried it out in a class, give feedback on the inventory website (www.ecml.at/ict-rev). By collaborating and sharing your experiences, the community of online teachers will grow and develop.

5 Why Does It Work?

This section will first make a case for integrating research and teaching more closely, then present some examples of research projects that have changed the way teachers feel about online teaching, and finally invite you to look at more research-based insights.

The task for this section is an invitation to try out action research in your own classes.

5.1 Different Forms of Research Relevant for Language Teachers

There is a suspicion among researchers that practitioners do not really engage with research papers or findings after their initial teacher training (Bartels, 2003; Kutlay, 2013). On the other hand, several teachers have voiced the concern that language teaching research misses the point and is not applicable in real-world classrooms (Allwright, 2003; Block 2000; Borg, 2009; Kutlay, 2013). From the beginning, this Element has attempted to reconcile the apparent gap and make research findings relevant for teachers while not ignoring the real needs and concerns of practitioners. There is no one-way transfer from research to teaching, claiming that 'researchers know best' and practitioners should just follow their advice. On the other hand, there is also no automatic involvement of practitioners in every research study that can produce pedagogically relevant insights. You will have to make your own decision on how much learning from others you want to engage with through (1) reading findings, summaries, and articles from specialist researchers; (2) practising with colleagues and online teacher communities; or – indeed – (3) learning from your learners. This sub-section will give some short examples of the first and second kind and invite you to participate in learning of the third kind in the task.

Language teaching research can take a variety of different forms, from evaluation of classroom experiences to lab-based experiments measured in controlled environments, and not everyone is agreed on what counts as research and what does not (Borg, 2009). If we start with what teachers practically and routinely do, the usual way of evaluating success of teaching takes two forms: firstly, evaluation of your students' progress is done through assessment; secondly, evaluation of your effect on students is measured through feedback. If we assume that all language teachers want their students to be successful in using the target language, and that, as expressed by one of the language teachers we surveyed recently, 'all teachers want to be popular with their students' (anonymous questionnaire response, 2021), these evaluations are often not done in the same spirit as research (i.e., being open to positive or negative outcomes, undertaken with a view to making the findings public and sharing them with a wider community for the purpose of improving knowledge or practice). Therefore, the routine classroom evaluations are labelled 'assessment' or 'evaluation' rather than research. The impressions of your standing in the view of your students are important and support reflection, personal development, and change. However, because of their intention they cannot help you when you are trying to find new ways of integrating technology into your teaching: students' evaluations are retrospective and subjective (i.e., students make their judgement after the teaching is over, sometimes only at the end of a semester or a course). Their evaluation is based on their own impression of your teaching, which can be influenced by their personal taste, general well-being, expectations, and success.

To generate more immediate and more concrete feedback, you can measure some effects of a new teaching strategy or method by using action research (Lewin, 1948). In action research, you select the element that should be evaluated, and you also select a suitable measure. Action research can take different forms, from quite simple evaluation (e.g., the suggested task at the end of this section) to rigorously conducted research projects (e.g., Fearn, 2021).

Action research is the most popular form of practitioner-based research, but different methodologies are used in educational research. In this section, I am going to select just a few examples of language teaching research in online contexts to demonstrate how we can establish a clearer understanding of online language teaching and how an integration of research findings can help language teachers in their day-to-day practice. I want to show not only that language teaching can be successful online but also that there is a value in linking the realms of teaching practice with teaching research more closely. The examples chosen here are:

a) a survey of language teachers to gauge the longer-term impact of ICT training on their practice
b) an action research cycle evaluating the effect of project-based language learning on students
c) a study of roles and scaffolding in online eTandem learning
d) an eye-tracking study supporting teacher reflection on the shared understanding they create with their students in an online tutorial.

These studies are not presented to prove a universal truth but to showcase the possibility of online language learning, whether through professional development, integrating online and offline elements, or through evidence that learning takes place in online synchronous environments.

5.2 Examples of Research Projects

If you have decided to consult this Element, presumably, you are already convinced that online language teaching works or has to work. After more than one year of enforced online teaching caused by lockdowns and social distancing rules, we would hope that there is some evidence for this or at least some positive examples. However, providing evidence that something works is more complicated than just collecting positive survey responses. We have to look at the concepts and terms used and decide for ourselves what a criterion for success would look like. Some researchers have been doing exactly that for the past decade. The following four examples of research investigating online language teaching and learning should provide some reassurance that our efforts in moving language teaching online with an appropriate and sustainable pedagogy have led to some success.

5.2.1 Survey

Surveys or questionnaires are a quick way of collecting responses from a large number of people. For evaluation of practice, online surveys can be useful. Supported by the ECML, the DOTS and ICT-REV teams have conducted workshops across Europe and beyond for more than 1,500 language teachers, training them to integrate online elements into their classroom teaching. Over the years, some of the teachers and organisers have come back to us, telling us how they have made use of the training and how they have progressed. The ECML regularly sent out feedback questionnaires straight after the end of the workshop and, again, six months later to evaluate the impact of our training. After almost ten years of workshops, we decided to conduct our own, longer-term impact evaluation. The team designed a questionnaire to be sent to former workshop participants and also asked for volunteers to be interviewed about their experience. Here are some of the findings from this evaluation.

A six-month follow-up questionnaire, sent to 138 workshop participants from Lithuania, Austria, Sweden, Spain, Ireland, and Bulgaria showed that 63.6 per cent indicated that they were using ICT tools and activities with more confidence and on a more frequent basis in the classroom. A significant 72.7 per cent indicated that they were using those ICT tools, activities, and ideas that had been presented in the workshop. Almost two-thirds of our participants (63.6 per cent) indicated that they had acted as a multiplier to promote the use of ICT tools and activities to others in the field. This cascading effect was a long-term impact we had hoped for. In another follow-up survey of seventy-seven participants who had attended workshops between 2013 and 2019 we found that more than two-thirds of participants, 68 per cent [n = 75] had gone on to develop their own materials using online tools, 82 per cent [n = 73] had worked with others to develop teaching materials, and 82 per cent [n = 58] had delivered training related to the DOTS framework to others.

These findings reveal that there is not only a short-term effect of training for online language teaching but also a longer-term impact, and sometimes also a cascading effect. The survey responses together with interviews and testimonials fed into an impact case study, evidencing the effects of tailor-made, participant-focussed ICT training on language teachers (Stickler et al., 2021; Stickler, Hampel & Emke, 2020).

This first example of systematic research shows how a survey can be used to collect data beyond immediate classroom evaluation. Although the publication was not peer-reviewed, its findings were made public and have helped us to reflect on and improve our practice as language teacher trainers.

5.2.2 Action Research

Action research is a practitioner-based enquiry that can help to check whether your own teaching works (Hampel, 2015; Noakes, n.d.). The action research cycle is based on Kurt Lewin's suggestion to involve practitioners in research to improve their situation (Lewin, 1948). It follows three or four steps: planning, implementing, evaluating, and re-designing, as shown in Figure 7. As every re-designing step can be seen as a new planning step, the cycle can turn into a spiral with an upward movement.

Language students benefit from a stay in the target-language country and, if possible, an immersion programme where they are encouraged to actively use the target language in communication with native or competent speakers.

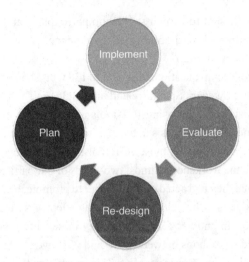

Figure 8 The action research cycle

Therefore, a period of residence abroad is part of many language courses in the United Kingdom. Because the Open University teaches courses part-time, at a distance, and most of our students are in employment, our 'period of residence' is very short: just one week. Students still benefit from the opportunity to use the language intensively; however, there are many students who cannot travel abroad. Some have health reasons, others have caring responsibilities, and some live in secure environments and are not allowed to leave. For these students we have created an online alternative to the week abroad. We call it the Alternative Learning Experience (ALE).

In 2020, together with two colleagues, I set up a small project to attempt to integrate the experience of students on our upper intermediate German course who were visiting a German town with the learning of those students who took part in the online alternative (see Stickler, StJohn, Kotschi, 2021). We used project-based language learning (Elam & Nesbit, 2012; Sampurna, 2019) as the pedagogical method, and implemented a '*Fotostrecke*', a type of *Instawalk* where we invited students to take photographs and write projects around their findings along specific intercultural themes. These photographs and projects were shared with students on the virtual equivalent of the exchange visit via the course website. This gave students who could not travel the opportunity to experience the visit virtually, second hand, mediated by technology and intro-duced by their peers. Using the materials collected by students in Germany, the students on the ALE also worked in groups to find additional information online, creating PowerPoint slides and presenting their projects in a public online session. Guests from the University of Jena and peers who had attended the residential school in Jena were invited as the audience, in addition to the full ALE cohort and their tutors.

This project-based ALE had already proven a success in 2020, as evidenced by evaluation data collected: employing digital tools and tasks, collaboration was enhanced, not only within the groups but also between the two formats of immersion. Where, previously, students on the ALE could have felt disadvantaged because their personal circumstances made it impossible for them to travel to Germany and experience cultural and linguistic immersion, the new format of the ALE provided an experience closer to a live visit and strengthened the collaborative aspect of their learning.

The real value of our innovative pedagogical approach, however, was revealed when, due to the COVID-19 pandemic, travel became impossible for all students in 2021. We created a one-week intensive ALE, mimicking immersion with a programme full of opportunities for collaboration, social online meetings, and visiting tutors from Jena. The programme ran fully online for one week in February 2021. Our pedagogic innovation has changed the way students engage with each other, learn to collaborate, and tolerate differences in ability and interest.

This example, like the first one, has also not been published as a research study (yet – we are still working on it). However, by sharing our findings with colleagues, we could influence online language teaching in the institution and have an impact on the experience of language students during COVID-19 restrictions.

5.2.3 eTandem and Alignment

The two examples in Sections 5.2.1 and 5.2.2 have shown that training can encourage teachers to use ICT in their teaching and that it might have unexpected benefits if they do so. However, looking at teachers and their experience does not actually tell us anything about the learning effects. We need to ask ourselves not only if we can move our teaching online but also whether students actually learn anything online, for example, in online discussions, chats, or tutorials. Several researchers have been investigating the benefits of eTandem learning and tried to show that – similar to face-to-face dialogues between native speakers and language learners – eTandems can also support language acquisition (Lewis, 2020; O'Dowd & Ritter, 2006; O'Rourke, 2007).

In a study of eTandem using video-conferencing software, Marco Cappellini (2016) researched four pairs of French and Chinese tandem partners, the roles they are taking and ascribing each other, and their attempts to help each other, or scaffold each other's learning. As mentioned, in tandem language learning the competent speaker of the language takes on the expert role, supporting the learning partner, the novice, in understanding and using the target language. As soon as the partners switch language, the role of expert is also switched around.

Cappellini shows that the role allocation is not quite as simple: The topic influences who is acting as expert or novice. When eTandem learners talk about a topic of their own culture in the target language, for example, the French partner speaking in Chinese about a French film, the roles of expert (in the culture) and novice (in the language) are reversed or 'crossed'. Cappellini's analysis shows that scaffolding – helping the less competent language partner – '. . . usually takes place when students present themselves as experts about their cultures and novices about the other's cultures' (Cappellini, 2016: 12). On the other hand, 'in crossed expertise configurations, a student combines the role of expert on the topic with that of learner of the language spoken, which leads mainly to scaffolding for her active vocabulary (lexical acquisition sequences)' (Cappellini, 2016: 16). Understanding these dynamics can help teachers and eTandem counsellors to create stimulating tasks and prepare suitable support materials.

Michel and Cappellini (2019) explored different configurations of online learning pairs to show how learners pick up linguistic habits of their interlocutors, whether in eTandems, or in textchat interaction with peers or language tutors (see also Michel & O'Rourke, 2019). This feature of communication called 'alignment' happens naturally when using one's first or preferred language, and has also been observed in language learners. Analysing this phenomenon in online communication has brought up interesting findings, for example, that structural alignment (i.e., a re-use or repetition of grammatical features of a language) happens more often in textchat than in video-conferencing mode. It might seem obvious that written interaction lends itself better to a focus on form. However, showing that this is the case in online communication gives language teachers a reason for choosing one mode (writing) over another (speaking) when creating tasks for particular learning outcomes.

5.2.4 Eye-Tracking

Another way to prove that online language learning can be effective, is to investigate what learners actually do while they are engaged in online interaction using eye-tracking. Eye-tracking shows where a person's gaze focus is while they are looking at a screen. It has been used for determining search patterns, for identifying points of interest in advertising, for improving the usability of web pages and – in applied linguistics – for reading research.

In online language teaching research, similar research questions have been investigated: Where do students focus their attention on a language teaching website? How do learners approach a text in a foreign language (Shen et al., 2012)? What are people looking for when attempting to answer test questions online (Bax, 2013)? When we narrow the field to synchronous online language learning, there are fewer studies (O'Rourke et al., 2015; Stickler & Shi, 2017), as the setting-up of research experiments becomes more complicated. Yet, eye-tracking can be useful when trying to convince people that online teaching can work. In a precursor study to Michel and Cappellini (2019), Marije Michel, together with Bryan Smith (Michel & Smith, 2017) used eye-tracking to investigate alignment in written textchat interaction. Eye-tracking could confirm that learners paid attention during some of the identified cases of lexical alignment, but the authors also warn us not to overestimate the cases of alignment simply based on textchat transcript.

Language teachers who are suddenly forced to take their teaching online, as was the case in the recent COVID-19 pandemic, for example, find themselves devoid of their usual means to establish shared understanding. The clues they take from learners' facial expressions, their focus or lack thereof, the gaze direction signalling attention or distraction, all those cues that an experienced language teacher in a classroom picks up and interprets without necessarily being aware of it, are missing. So how do we know in an online learning environment that learners are paying attention? The fear of talking or teaching into the void is particularly pertinent for language teachers who are trying to help their learners use the best possible means for communication.

In an attempt to prove to language teachers that learners online follow their guidance and share the understanding of a 'learning space', we (Shi & Stickler, 2021) set up an experiment, tracking the gaze movements of a learner and teacher simultaneously. We set up two eye-trackers in different rooms, recording the eye movements of the teacher and one learner out of the student group during online language teaching sessions. After the eye-tracking experiment, the teacher and learner both watched the gaze plot videos together and commented on the experience and their intentions and strategies. The study served not only to show that learners follow their online language teacher's instructions and intended teaching points, but also to reassure the participating teachers that their efforts did not go unnoticed and their use of pointers, virtual and verbal, were successful.

5.3 Continuing Research

There are many more studies that could be of interest to language teachers, and many are being added every year. If you started with the task in Section 2, you may already have found a way to keep abreast of new developments. If not, you could also select one of the leading journals in this area, for example, *CALICO*, *CALL*, *China CALL*, *JALT CALL*, *Language Learning and Technology*, *ReCALL*, or *System*. You can search for a relevant article in the journals, or use online repositories of freely accessible academic work (e.g., ORO (http://oro.open.ac.uk/), UCL Discovery (https://discovery.ucl.ac.uk/), or Archives Ouvertes (https://hal.archives-ouvertes.fr/)).

5.4 Task

As a task for this section, it seems appropriate to suggest action research. Evaluation is an integral part of every teacher's practice, and by using a few techniques, a simple class evaluation can turn into a mini-research project.

To start your own action research mini-project, focus on one element of your technology use in language teaching that you feel really confident with – for example the use of YouTube videos to show authentic language input. Set yourself an evaluation measure (e.g., the uptake of students' re-use of language elements from this input). Count the number of times your students re-use a particular phrase or language structure in their own essays or speaking tasks. If you are satisfied, count it as a win and congratulate yourself and your students. If you find that the re-use of language elements is not particularly high, develop a new task that challenges students to identify, recognise, analyse, or re-use the language element in a new video input. Repeat the action research cycle until you are satisfied.

When you feel confident with your technology use, start more ambitious action research cycles or spirals. You can also read up on other researchers' studies based on this method or you can form teams with your colleagues, share particular tasks and evaluation methods, and start comparing your results.

6 Future-Proofing Our Language Teaching

This final section will start with a reference to the COVID-19 crisis – a stark reminder that online communication might not always be a choice for teachers. It will then present five vignettes of possible futures for language teaching professionals, based on a subjective interpretation of qualitative survey responses. It will briefly digress into a pessimistic view of the future of language teaching before ending with a personal – and optimistic – outlook.

The task for this section is reflective, evaluative, and prepares you for further self-training and professional development.

6.1 Nobody Expects . . . the Unexpected

In February 2020, just before the first lockdown of the pandemic changed the way schools across Europe and the world delivered their teaching, I was in

Germany for a small research study. For details of the study, see Section 5. As mentioned, this small research project proved very beneficial when, in 2021, all visits and international travel had to be cancelled and all students had to make do with a virtual, but media-rich, visit to Germany. In a way, it proved to be a serendipitous future-proofing of our German course.

The COVID-19 crisis has shown that online or distance teaching is possible, if not always as successful as the teachers would hope. Language teaching is moving online, not only because of enforced lockdowns, social distancing, and school closures, but also because communication is moving more and more online and in the direction of being mediated through technology. The same way that language itself changes over time and adapts to new communication habits (Seargeant, 2021), language teaching needs to adapt. As online and blended teaching is a development that will be of growing importance in the coming years, this Element – together with other resources (see the list at the end of this Element) provides some support to make the upcoming and foreseeable changes more successful and enjoyable. Being aware of the likelihood of change can make us more flexible, resilient, and give us choice, rather than the feeling of being driven by external forces.

In the next sub-section, I will speculate about some future developments in language teaching and communication practices. Parts of this section are based on research undertaken with the team of the TPLang21 Research Network (https://aila.info/research/list-of-rens/perspectives-and-trajectories-of-lan guage-teacher/), a network of more than forty researchers from nineteen coun- tries supported by AILA, the Association Internationale de Linguistique Appliquée or International Association of Applied Linguistics, who investigate the perspectives and trajectories of language teachers with regard to technology use.

6.2 Language Teachers of the Future

At the end of the year 2020, our research group invited language teachers from ten different countries to brainstorm about language teaching in the 2030s, with 109 responding (Germain-Rutherford et al., 2021). In the middle of a pandemic and after ten months of experience of online or distance teaching, our research participants described their visions of the future of language teaching in very different ways. I have created vignettes based on the English translations of eighty-seven valid responses[5]; and I will present five teacher types here,

---

[5] With heartfelt thanks to Aline Germain-Rutherford, Tibor Pinter, and Patricia Vasconcelos Almeida, as well as DeepL and Google Translate, for the translation from the French, Hungarian, and Portuguese.

together with some verbatim quotes to outline several options for future language teachers ten or more years down the line.

1) The first type or vignette is the Visionary: A language teacher embracing technology with enthusiasm, they welcome the opportunity to experiment not only with new tools and media but also with pedagogic innovation. This teacher talks about the future with curiosity and openness, enhanced by knowledge rooted in current developments. Learning from the learners is an integral part of their role, and change is part of their life. In her own voice, this teacher thinks: 'In ten years I believe (and hope) that a majority of English teachers around the globe are working with projects and virtual exchange. That will make my role as a teacher easier' (anonymous questionnaire response, 2021, English)

2) The Traditionalist: A different type of language teacher, they value the tried and tested methods for language teaching, and emphasise traditional skills, such as an expertise in the target language or accuracy in grammatical forms. This teacher is particularly looking forward to a return to face-to-face teaching: 'I don't think that ICT can completely replace face-to-face teaching with a teacher, although, willy-nilly, I use it a lot these days' (anonymous questionnaire response, 2021, French). On the other hand, very often recognising that teaching also requires emotional support, this teacher might also long for the opportunity to provide the human face of teaching that they feel is lacking in the online environment.

3) The Designer: The future of language teaching might well be in designing materials and learning environments, creating opportunities for language learners to learn as independently and autonomously as possible: 'I envision my role mainly as a process manager and evaluator' (anonymous questionnaire response, 2021, Hungarian). The teacher as an expert is definitely stepping back from the limelight in this scenario. This teacher includes fun and games as elements of language teaching and does not mind taking a back seat once the design stage has been completed.

4) The Mediator: Teachers have already started curating content from a variety of sources. As supporters and organisers of eTandem learning, they are brokering communication opportunities rather than explicitly teaching the target language. Many teachers welcome this chance to become mediators and facilitators rather than the 'sage on the stage' of old. For example, this enthusiastic German language teacher: 'I am a facilitator and learning guide. I offer my expertise mainly in the organisation of the learning units' (anonymous questionnaire response, 2021,

German). For a language teacher, mediating cultural differences is also part of the task. This type of language teacher finds resources online, evaluates and vets them and recommends the best for their students' use. The development of this mediation role is made possible through the OER movement, the free sharing of OERs, open educational practices (OEPs), and the recommendation and cataloguing of open and free online tools.

5) The Critical Voice: Some language teachers see their role as going beyond the teaching of just language or culture; they take into account social issues and aim at making students aware of the wider world. This type of teacher identifies the impact of new technologies on society and wants to develop this critical awareness in their students as well. From a Brazilian context, one teacher's voice exemplifies the type by claiming 'sensitivity to students' needs and the critical issues of the socio-economic, political and historical context, critical reflection on the affordances of recent technologies' (anonymous questionnaire response, 2021, Portuguese), as the necessary qualities of a language teacher. Critical citizens, independent thinkers, mature and responsible adults – no less is the goal this language teacher wants to achieve.

These five vignettes show some of the directions our profession can take in the future. Awareness of upcoming societal change can help us to future-proof not only our individual teaching practice by training for online and blended teaching, but also the profession as a whole. For example, if we recognise now that OERs are already used in language teaching (Daniels, 2021), and will become even more important in the future, we need to start acknowledging the role of a curator of OER content and mediator of OEPs as integrative for language teaching. Future language teachers need to be trained facilitators, mediators, and curators, and educational establishments need to acknowledge these skills as necessary for teaching. Otherwise, language teaching in this new form might become a labour of love rather than a recognised and financially viable profession.

Finally, and to conclude the findings from our questionnaire study (Germain-Rutherford et al., 2021), it is worth mentioning one more option: the disappearance of the language teacher altogether. The fear that our role might become superfluous has been around at least as long as CALL studies have been conducted, and the advance of AI has only increased the concerns. Mirroring Godwin-Jones' speculations (2019), some of our respondents mention that teaching as a role might become superfluous, as students, with the help of automated systems, can learn independently and be assessed automatically. The frustration of being forced to move language teaching online has already prompted a number of teachers to consider retirement from the profession altogether, and others dismiss the need to engage in a changing profession ('I will be retired in 2030' (anonymous questionnaire response, 2021, French)).

6.3 No Future

This entire Element has been written under the assumption that there will be people in the future who will want to learn a language, and to some degree, that there will also be a need for language teachers. It is driven by optimism and a fundamental belief that languages are not just simple means of communication but that they transport worldviews and cultures. If language is only taken in its ancillary use, there are valid considerations that language learning will lose meaning in the future: either because of the hegemony of one language or a very small number of languages, or because technology will be so proficient in quickly translating and interpreting between different languages that the simple extrinsic motivation of being able to use different languages for these purposes will be lost. In both these scenarios, it would not make sense to waste time learning a language to communicate for business purposes, for example. If we can use machine translation not only to facilitate a basic grasp of texts in a foreign language but also to produce output texts in that language, why bother learning a language at all (Henshaw, 2020)? If something like a babel fish (Adams, 1995) can replace the services of a simultaneous interpreter, why learn this difficult skill?

In his answer to the question why learning another language might still be useful or necessary 'In a World of SMART Technology', Robert Godwin-Jones (2019) describes three scenarios: a technology so smart that it can instantaneously translate and interpret spoken and written language and language variants into other languages for the interlocutors; an Internet so rich in resources that language learning can happen spontaneously and without guided instruction; and a third scenario, where language teaching is still valuable but shifts its emphasis from its ancillary usefulness to trade and commerce to a cultural appreciation of diversity and global citizenship. I share his view and add that neither a purported language hegemony nor technological advances will be able to respond satisfactorily to questions such as: How will the diversity of cultures, of mindsets, and views of the world be represented in one (fictional) mega-language? How will abilities such as empathetic understanding, and attitudes such as a tolerance of ambiguity be engendered if not through the realisation of a diversity of languages and cultures?

6.4 A Future with Technology

In my view there will be a need for language teaching and language teachers in the future but teaching without technology will become obsolete and not acceptable to future generations of learners. The answer to technological advances is not to ban technology from the classroom but to embrace it and integrate it into the practice of language teaching. We as language teachers need to be prepared to adapt to a world of online communication and make our expertise explicit, not only in the target language and metalinguistic knowledge but also in empathy and meaning making and in our ability to engender an attitude of openness and enquiry (Byram, 1997) in our learners and to teach communication skills beyond the skill of transfer and translation between languages.

As we have seen from the vignettes of language teachers of the future, the decision is ours. There is not just one option of how we can re-define the profession. As critical pedagogues, we will point out that the vision of a 'world language' carries with it the dangers of neo-colonialism and discuss the threats to identity entailed in this (see, e.g., Sandhu & Higgins, 2016). Language teachers know better than other professionals the richness a plurality of languages can bring; and European institutions like the ECML explicitly support multilingual and plurilingual lives and education. And last but not least, we are aware that our ontological beliefs – ingrained in our teaching values – may influence whether we appreciate or deplore the simplicity of one answer, one language, one truth. As long as our ontology does not allow the one, fixed reality, as long as our epistemology questions the concept of one ideal truth, any claim of creating a neutral means of communication must fail.

Hence, this Element is based on optimism; on a belief that democratic resistance against neo-colonial language hegemony will be sufficient to keep a diversity of languages alive and – more than just surviving – thriving as a valid and appreciated subject for study. It also implies optimism on the part of teacher trainers and pedagogues: the belief that future language teachers will take on the challenge of technological advances and use technology in their teaching to support the difficult task of learning a new language, a new culture, and a new perspective on the world. This takes courage and commitment. Finally, this Element was written in the hope that it can be a useful aide to those courageous and committed individuals who will still be teaching languages in ten, twenty or thirty years' time.

Table 4 Grid for planning your self-training activities.

Target (what?)	Current knowledge / skill (now?)	Aim (future knowledge / skill?)	Steps (how?)	Checking success (evaluate?)	Obstacles (why not?)	Timing (when?)	Rewards (why?)
1							
2							
3							
4							

Table 5 Sample table for self-training plan

Characteristics of the role	Needed skills	Example of training activity
Awareness of OERs	Finding, identifying, vetting OER	a) Peer-supported online search for a good repository of language-specific OERs
	Advanced skill:	b) Joining an online OER group to remix / repurpose OER
Supporting eTandem learning	Finding eTandem partners, creating eTandem learning tasks, coaching or counselling eTandem learners	a) Enrolling in a Virtual Exchange network (e.g., EVOLVE: https://evolve-erasmus.eu/about-evolve/), following an online training course for language teachers supporting virtual exchanges
	Advanced interest:	b) Attending a conference on virtual exchange and eTandem learning

6.5 Task

6.5.1 Part 1

Reflection

Start by reflecting on your reactions to the vignettes of possible future language teachers earlier in this section. How did they make you feel? Was there one that frightened you? Encouraged you? Made you curious and motivated?

Choose a vignette that you can relate to.

Choose a task or an activity that you use frequently in your language teaching (face-to-face or online). Now imagine what this task or activity could look like in ten years' time with the advance of technology. Follow the guidance of your chosen vignette and re-write the activity radically.

For example, if you chose a listening activity, you could make it into an online freely chosen video-watching activity where students employ automatic captioning and – if they need it – also on-the-spot translation and subtitling. Consider what skills the students will need and what benefit they will gain from employing this additional technology.

6.5.2 Part 2

Forward Planning

As a second step to this final task, make a plan for your future (self-)training activities. What kind of continuing professional development will you need for your preferred future teaching role? Consider development, learning, and training in small steps. You can either use the grid in Table 4 for step-by-step guidance, or the simpler grid filled in as an example in Table 5 or you can design your own training plan.

To give you one example, Table 5 is based on the vignette of the mediator and entails some characteristics, skills and activities.

Glossary

Affordances: James Gibson (1904–79) used this term to describe a form of interaction between the environment and the individual, where the individual can take advantage of what the environment offers only if they perceive its potential.

Authenticity: A highly debated term in language teaching, as authentic language use can be defined through actual use by competent speakers; common use by a majority of speakers; or every kind of language use that happens without script.

Blended teaching: The systematic combination of face-to-face and online elements to enhance the learning experience. New terms like HyFlex teaching also include the simultaneous use of online and face-to-face teaching from the same classroom.

Competent speaker: To replace the notion of 'native speaker' and its associated meaning and post-colonial attitude, the term 'competent speaker' is used to denote an L1 speaker who can use the target language up to a level that she is able to teach it. Proficient speaker is also used.

CALL Computer-assisted language learning. Different terms, for example TELL (technology-enhanced language learning), are sometimes used.

DOTS: Developing Online Teaching Skills. A collaborative teacher training project supported by the ECML.

ECML: European Centre for Modern Languages. A division of the Council of Europe, concerned with supporting language teachers and policy-makers across Europe. With thirty-four member states it covers a wider area than the European Union. www.ecml.at/Aboutus/AboutUs-Overview/tabid/172/language/en-GB/Default.aspx

Epistemology: A branch of philosophy that seeks to understand how we know.

eTandem: Any form of tandem language learning that uses electronic means. Different terms, such as teletandem, email tandem or telecollaboration are used by different researchers.

Face-to-face: Teaching and learning in the physical presence of both learner and teacher.

Flipped pedagogy (Flipped classroom): A pedagogy that uses synchronous interaction mainly to discuss concepts and theories learned outside of the classroom. Teachers prepare the content for students to learn before the concept is then activated and discussed during class time.

ICT Information and communication technology.

Interlocutor A person (or non-human entity) to whom the communication is directed whether in written or spoken conversation, in online communication, or face-to-face. In online language learning this could be a chat-bot, as well as a teacher or an eTandem partner.

L2: Second or additional language.

MOOC: Massive open online course. Originally designed as free learning materials, MOOCs are aimed at independent learners who can select and access pedagogically structured online materials, mostly without teacher support. Platforms include: Coursera, edX, FutureLearn, and Udacity.

OER: Open educational resources, also OEPs (open educational practices). An educational movement advocating free access to educational resources for all, expressed in the Paris declaration: https://en.unesco.org/oer/paris-declaration.

Online: Using digital tools (e.g., networked computers, mobile devices, etc.), to access information or to communicate over a WiFi or internet connection.

Ontology: A branch of philosophy that deals with the very basis of existence, the being of things.

Sapir-Whorf hypothesis: Edward Sapir (1884–1939) and Benjamin Lee Whorf (1897–1941) researched how the language someone uses impacts on their thinking. They formulated the hypothesis that language influences or shapes thought.

STAR structure: Using the structuring elements of Space, Time, Accreditation, and Role to describe differences in how a language course is set up, managed, and perceived (see Section 1).

Three Axes framework: Based on the work by Lijing Shi and Ursula Stickler (2019), this framework places technology use in language teaching on three axes or dimensions of a cube: visibility of technology, authenticity of communication, and teacher intervention. It allows language teachers to position their actual or intended technology use and align it with their pedagogic aims.

Target language: The language that is being learned. It now also includes the target culture, target-language behaviour, etc.

VLE: Virtual learning environment. Also known as Course Management System or Learning Management System. A platform that allows teachers and schools to collect and manage tasks set by teacher, work submitted by students, and often also the administration of assessment. Open Source examples are Moodle and Sakai.

Platforms, Apps, and Tools

Open Access academic research publications:

Archives Ouvertes https://hal.archives-ouvertes.fr/
ORO: Open Research Online oro.open.ac.uk
UCL (University College London) Discovery https://discovery.ucl.ac.uk/

Academic research search engines:

Google Scholar: https://scholar.google.co.uk/
Mendeley: www.mendeley.com/

Tools:

Blabberize: https://blabberize.com/make
DeepL: www.deepl.com/translator
eTwinning: www.facebook.com/ETwinningeurope
Facebook: www.facebook.com/
Google Translate: translate.google.com
Instagram: www.instagram.com
Kahoot: https://kahoot.it/
Padlet: https://padlet.com/
Skype: www.skype.com/en/
SurveyMonkey: www.surveymonkey.com/
Twitter: https://twitter.com/
WhatsApp: www.whatsapp.com
YouTube: www.youtube.com/

Collections:

Dig.Comp.Edu 2.0 (2016): The Digital Competence Framework: https://ec
.europa.eu/jrc/en/digcomp/digital-competence-framework

Toolkit: OpenLearn Create (2020) Moving your language teaching online – a toolkit. Available at: www.open.edu/openlearncreate/course/view.php?id=6341

Inventory of online tools and Open Educational Resources (2015). European Centre for Modern Languages (ECML). Available at: www.ecml.at/ict-rev

References

Adams, D. (1995). *The Hitchhiker's Guide to the Galaxy: A Trilogy in Five Parts*. London: Random House.

Allwright, D. (2003). Exploratory Practice: Rethinking Practitioner Research in Language Teaching. *Language Teaching Research*, 7(2), 113–41.

Androutsopoulos, J. (2011). Language Change and Digital Media: A Review of Conceptions and Evidence. *Standard Languages and Language Standards in a Changing Europe*, 1, 145–59.

Austin, J. L. (1962). *How to Do Things With Words*. Oxford: Oxford University Press.

Aydin, S. (2016). Webquests as Language-Learning Tools. *Computer Assisted Language Learning*, 29(4), 765–78. https://doi.org/10.1080/09588221.2015.1061019.

Bartels, N. (2003). How Teachers and Researchers Read Academic Articles. *Teaching and Teacher Education*, 19(7), 737–53.

Batardière, M. T., and Jeanneau, C. (2020). Towards Developing Tandem Learning in Formal Language Education. Recherche et pratiques pédagogiques en langues de spécialité. *Cahiers de l'Apliut*, 39(1). https://journals.openedition.org/apliut/7842.

Bax, S. (2003). CALL – Past, Present and Future. *System*, 31(1), 13–28. https://doi.org/10.1016/s0346-251x(02)00071-4.

Bax, S. (2011). Normalisation Revisited: The Effective Use of Technology in Language Education. *International Journal of Computer-Assisted Language Learning and Teaching (IJCALLT)*, 1(2), 1–15.

Bax, S. (2013). The Cognitive Processing of Candidates During Reading Tests: Evidence from Eye-Tracking. *Language Testing*, 30(4), 441–65.

Block, D. (2000). Revisiting the Gap between SLA Researchers and Language Teachers. *Links & Letters*, (7), 129–43.

Borg, S. (2009). English Language Teachers' Conceptions of Research. *Applied Linguistics*, 30(3), 358–88.

Brammerts, H. (1996). Language Learning in Tandem Using the Internet. In M. Warschauer (ed.), *Telecollaboration in Foreign Language Learning: Proceedings of the Hawaii Symposium*, vol. 12. Honolulu: University of Hawai'i Second Language Teaching and Curriculum Center, 121–30.

Brammerts, L. (2003). Autonomous Language Learning in Tandem: The Development of a Concept. In T. Lewis and L. Walker (eds.), *Autonomous*

Language Learning in Tandem. Sheffield: Academy Electronic Publications, 27–36.

Byram, M. (1997). *Teaching and Assessing Intercultural Communicative Competence*. Clevedon, UK: Multilingual Matters.

Bytheway, J. (2015). A Taxonomy of Vocabulary Learning Strategies Used in Massively Multiplayer Online Role-Playing Games. *CALICO Journal*, 32 (3), 508–27.

Cappellini, M. (2016). Roles and Scaffolding in Teletandem Interactions: A Study of the Relations between the Sociocultural and the Language Learning Dimensions in a French–Chinese Teletandem. *Innovation in Language Learning and Teaching*, 10(1), 6–20.

Coleman, J. A., Hampel, R., Hauck, M., and Stickler, U. (2010). Collaboration and Interaction: The Keys to Distance and Computer-Supported Language Learning. In G. Levine, and A. S. Phipps (eds.), *Critical and Intercultural Theory and Language Pedagogy*. Boston: Heinle, 161–80.

Comas-Quinn, A. (2011). Learning to Teach Online or Learning to Become an Online Teacher: An Exploration of Teachers' Experiences in a Blended Learning Course. *ReCALL*, 23(03), 218–32.

Compernolle, R. A. van, and Williams, L. (2013). Sociocultural Theory and Second Language Pedagogy. *Language Teaching Research*, 17(3), 277–81. https://doi.org/10.1177/1362168813482933.

Cziko, G. A. (2004). Electronic Tandem Language Learning (eTandem): A Third Approach to Second Language Learning for the 21st Century. *CALICO Journal*, 22(1), 25–40.

Daniels, P. (2021). 'A Case Study Exploring Freelance English Language Teachers' Engagement with and Informal Learning through Open Educational Practices in Switzerland'. EdD thesis. The Open University.

Deleuze, G., and Guattari, F. (1987). *A Thousand Plateaus: Capitalism and Schizophrenia*. Vancouver/Minneapolis: University of Minnesota.

Denzin, N. K. (2009). The Elephant in the Living Room: Or Extending the Conversation about the Politics of Evidence. *Qualitative Research*, 9(2), 139–60.

Derrida, J. (1972). *Die Schrift und die Differenz*. Frankfurt: Suhrkamp.

Develotte, C., Guichon, N., and Vincent, C. (2010). The Use of the Webcam for Teaching a Foreign Language in a Desktop Videoconferencing Environment. *ReCALL*, 22(3), 293–312.

Downes, S. (2019). Recent Work in Connectivism. *European Journal of Open, Distance and E-Learning* (EURODL), 22(2), 113–32.

Elam, J. R., and Nesbit, B. (2012). The Effectiveness of Project-Based Learning Utilizing Web2.0 Tools in EFL. *JALTCALL Journal*, 8(2), 113–27.

Ellis, R. (2003). *Task-Based Language Learning and Teaching*. Oxford: Oxford University Press.

Ernest, P., and Heiser, S. (In press). Teacher Training in Times of Covid. In U. Stickler and M. Emke (eds.), *Online Language Teaching: Crises and Creativities*. London: Castledown.

Ertmer, P. A., and Ottenbreit-Leftwich, A. T. (2010). Teacher Technology Change: How Knowledge, Confidence, Beliefs, and Culture Intersect. *Journal of Research on Technology in Education*, 42(3), 255–84.

Fearn, L. J. (2021). 'An Enquiry into English as a Foreign Language and Online Community Projects in Secondary School Education'. EdD thesis. The Open University.

Fischer, R. (2007). How Do We Know What Students Are Actually Doing? Monitoring Students' Behavior in CALL. *Computer Assisted Language Learning*, 20(5), 409–42.

Freire, P. (1996). *Pedagogy of the Oppressed* (revised). New York: Continuum.

Freud, S. (1900). *Die Traumdeutung*. Leipzig/Vienna: Franz Deuticke.

Gasser, M. (1990). Connectionism and Universals of Second Language Acquisition. *Studies in Second Language Acquisition*, 12(2), 179–99.

Germain-Rutherford, A., and Ernest, P. (2015). European Language Teachers and ICT: Experiences, Expectations and Training Needs. In R. Hampel and U. Stickler (eds.), *Developing Online Language Teaching*. London: Palgrave Macmillan, 12–27.

Germain-Rutherford, A., Stickler U., Hampel, R. et al. (2021). Language Teachers in the 21st Century: Perspectives and Trajectories. Featured symposium presentation. AILA 2021, Groningen and online. 15–20 August. https://aila2021.dryfta.com/program/program/128/s139-ren-language-teachers-in-the-21st-century-perspectives-and-trajectories.

Gibson, J. J. (1979). The Theory of Affordances. In J. J. Gibson, *The Ecological Approach to Visual Perception*. Boston: Houghton Mifflin, 127–36.

Glasersfeld, E. von (2007). *Key Works in Radical Constructivism* (M. Larochelle, ed.). Rotterdam: Sense Publishers.

Godwin-Jones, R. (2009). Speech Tools and Technologies. *Language Learning & Technology*, 13(3), 4–11.

Godwin-Jones, R. (2015). The Evolving Roles of Language Teachers: Trained Coders, Local Researchers, Global Citizens. *Language Learning & Technology*, 19(1), 10–22.

Godwin-Jones, R. (2019). In a World of SMART Technology, Why Learn Another Language? *Journal of Educational Technology & Society*, 22(2), 4–13.

Goodier, T., Germain-Rutherford, A., Laurence, G., and Piccardo, E. (2021). A Platform for Celebrating Plurilingualism – Insights from the Lincdire LITE

E-Portfolio Project. Conference presentation. AILA 2021, Groningen and online. 15–20 August. https://aila2021.dryfta.com/program/program/128/s139-ren-lan guage-teachers-in-the-21st-century-perspectives-and-trajectories.

Hampel, R. (2015). Theoretical Approaches and Research-Based Pedagogies for Online Teaching. In R. Hampel and U. Stickler (eds.), *Developing Online Language Teaching*. London: Palgrave Macmillan, 134–49.

Hampel, R. (2019). *Disruptive Technologies and the Language Classroom*. London: Springer International Publishing.

Hampel, R., and de los Arcos, B. (2013). Interacting at a Distance: A Critical Review of the Role of ICT in Developing the Learner–Context Interface in a University Language Programme. *Innovation in Language Learning and Teaching*, 7(2), 158–78.

Hampel, R., Germain-Rutherford, A., and Stickler, U. (2014). The Need for Training in Online Language Teaching. Presentation at the AILA 2014 conference in Brisbane, Australia. 10–14 August.

Hampel, R., and Stickler, U. (2005). New Skills for New Classrooms. Training Tutors to Teach Languages Online. *Computer Assisted Language Learning*, 18(4), 311–26.

Hampel, R., and Stickler, U. (2012). The Use of Videoconferencing to Support Multimodal Interaction in an Online Language Classroom. *ReCALL*, 24(2), 116–37. https://doi.org/10.1017/S095834401200002X.

Hanna, B., and De Nooy, J. (2003). A Funny Thing Happened on the Way to the Forum: Electronic Discussion and Foreign Language Learning. *Language Learning & Technology*, 7(1), 71–85.

Heath, P., and Carroll, L. (1974). *The Philosopher's Alice: Alice's Adventures in Wonderland & Through the Looking-glass*. New York: Saint Martin's.

Heins, B., Duensing, A., Stickler, U., and Batstone, C. (2007). Spoken Interaction in Online and Face-to-Face Language Tutorials. *Computer Assisted Language Learning*, 20(3), 279–95.

Heiser, S., Stickler, U., and Furnborough, C. (2013). Student Training in the Use of an Online Synchronous Conferencing Tool. *CALICO Journal*, 30(2), 226–51.

Henshaw, F. (2020). Online Translators in Language Classes: Pedagogical and Practical Considerations. *The FLTmag.com*. Online. 15 July . https://fltmag .com/online-translators-pedagogical-practical-considerations/ (last accessed 14 September 2021).

Holec, H. (1981). *Autonomy and Foreign Language Learning*. Oxford: Pergamon Press.

Hu, Z., and McGrath, I. (2011). Innovation in Higher Education in China: Are Teachers Ready to Integrate ICT in English language Teaching? *Technology, Pedagogy and Education*, 20(1), 41–59.

Illich, I. (1970). *De-schooling Society.* New York: Harper and Row.

Irigaray, L. (1980). *Speculum: Spiegel des anderen Geschlechts.* Frankfurt: Suhrkamp.

Jung, U. O. H. (2005). CALL: Past, Present and Future – A Bibliometric Approach. *ReCALL*, 17(1), 4–17.

Kan, Q. (2013). The Use of ICT in Supporting Distance Chinese Language Learning – Review of the Open University's Beginners' Chinese Course. *Technology and Chinese Language Teaching*, 4(1), 1–13.

Kern, R., Ware, P., and Warschauer, M. (2008). Network-Based Language Teaching. In S. May and N. H. Hornberger, eds., *Encyclopedia of Language and Education*, vol. 4, 281–92. https://doi.org/10.1007/978-0-387-30424-3_105.

Kincheloe, J. L. (2005). *Critical Constructivism.* New York/Washington, DC: Peter Lang.

Koenraad, T. (2006). LanguageQuest Design and Telecollaboration. *Teaching English with Technology*, 6(3).

Kop, R., and Hill, A. (2008). Connectivism: Learning Theory of the Future or Vestige of the Past? *International Review of Research in Open and Distance Learning*, 9(3), 1–13. https://doi.org/10.19173/irrodl.v9i3.523.

Krämer, S. (2010). Was sind Kulturtechniken? Kleines Plädoyer für ein 'Handwerk des Geistes', *Schulmagazin 5-10. Impulse für kreativen Unterricht.* Heft 9, 2010, 7–11.

Kutlay, N. (2013). A Survey of English Language Teachers' Views of Research. *Procedia-Social and Behavioral Sciences*, 70, 188–206.

Lantolf, J. P. (2000). Introducing Sociocultural Theory. In J. P. Lantolf (ed.), *Sociocultural Theory and Second Language Learning.* Oxford: Oxford University Press, 1–26.

Lantolf, J. P., Thorne, S. L., and Poehner, M. E. (2014). Sociocultural Theory and Second Language Development. In B. van Patten and J. Williams (eds.), *Theories in Second Language Acquisition.* New York: Routledge, 207–26. https://doi.org/10.4324/9780203628942-16.

Levy, M., and Hubbard, P. (2005). Why Call CALL 'CALL'? *Computer Assisted Language Learning*, 18(3), 143–9. https://doi.org/10.1080/09588220500208884.

Lewin, K. (1948). *Resolving Social Conflicts.* Selected papers on group dynamics. New York: Harper.

Lewis, T. (2004). The Effective Learning of Languages in Tandem. In J. A. Coleman and J. Klapper (eds.), *Effective Learning and Teaching in Modern Languages.* London: Routledge, 179–86.

Lewis, T. (2006). When Teaching is Learning: A Personal Account of Learning to Teach Online, *CALICO Journal*, 23(3), 581–600.

Lewis, T. (2020). From Tandem Learning to E-Tandem Learning: How Languages Are Learnt in Tandem Exchanges. In S. Gola, M. Pierrard, E. Tops, and D. Van Raemdonck (eds.), *Enseigner et apprendre les langues au XXIe siècle*. Méthodes alternatives et nouveaux dispositifs d'accompagnement. GRAMM-R. Brussels: P.I.E. Peter Lang.

Lewis, T., and Walker, L. (2003). *Autonomous Language Learning in Tandem*. Sheffield: Academy Electronic Press.

Li, C. (Chenxi). (2021). Negotiating for Meaning in Audio- and Video Synchronous Computer Mediated Communication. PhD thesis. The Open University.

Lindeiner-Stráský, K. von, Barkanyi, Zs., Gargett, A., et al. (2021). An Investigation into Web-Based Machine Translation (WBMT) in the Use of Digital Language Learning, Teaching, and Assessment. Final project report. Internal document. The Open University.

Lindeiner-Stráský, K. von, Pulker, H., and Vialleton, E. (In press). 'Moving Your Language Teaching Online' Toolkit: Teachers' Early Reflections on their Experience and Skills. In U. Stickler and M. Emke (eds.), *Online Language Teaching: Crises and Creativities*. London: Castledown.

Lindeiner-Stráský, K. von, Stickler, U., and Winchester, S. (2020). Flipping the Flipped. The Concept of Flipped Learning in an Online Teaching Environment. *Open Learning: The Journal of Open, Distance and e-Learning*, 1–17.

Little, D. (2001). Learner Autonomy and the Challenge of Tandem Language Learning via the Internet. In A. Chambers and G. Davies (eds.), *ICT and Language Learning: A European Perspective*. Lisse: Swets & Zeitlinger, 29–38.

Lund, A., Furberg, A., Bakken, J., and Engelien, K. L. (2014). What Does Professional Digital Competence Mean in Teacher Education? *Nordic Journal of Digital Literacy*, 9(4), 280–98.

Mezirow, J. (1981). A Critical Theory of Adult Learning and Education. *Adult Learning*, 32(1), 3–24.

Michel, M., and Cappellini, M. (2019). Alignment During Synchronous Video Versus Written Chat L2 Interactions: A Methodological Exploration. *Annual Review of Applied Linguistics*, 39, 189–216.

Michel, M., and O'Rourke, B. (2019). What Drives Alignment During Text Chat with a Peer vs. a Tutor? Insights from Cued Interviews and Eye-Tracking. *System*, 83, 50–63.

Michel, M., and Smith, B. (2017). Measuring Lexical Alignment during L2 Chat Interaction: An Eye-Tracking Study. In S. M. Gass, A. Mackey, P. Spinner, and J. Behney (eds.), *Salience in Second Language Acquisition*. London: Routledge, 244–68.

Millwood, R. (2013). *Learning Theory*. Online resource. Blog entry (10 May). https://blog.richardmillwood.net/2013/05/10/learning-theory/.

Mitchell, R., Myles, F., and Marsden, E. (2019). *Second Language Learning Theories*. London: Routledge.

Noakes, N. (n.d.). *Getting Started with Action Research*. Online resource. http://cei.hkust.edu.hk/teaching-resources/action-research.

O'Dowd, R., and Ritter, M. (2006). Understanding and Working with 'Failed Communication' in Telecollaborative Exchanges. *CALICO Journal*, 23(3), 623–42.

OECD (2018). *TALIS 2018 Results*: Teachers and School Leaders as Lifelong Learners (Volume I). OECD Library. https://doi.org/10.1787/1d0bc92a-en.

O'Rourke, B. (2007). Models of Telecollaboration (1): eTandem. In R. O'Dowd (ed.), *Online Intercultural Exchange. An Introduction for Foreign Language Teachers*. Clevedon: Multilingual Matters, 41–61.

O'Rourke, B., Prendergast, C., Shi, L., Smith, B., and Stickler, U. (2015). Eyetracking in CALL–present and future. In A. M. G. Sanz, M. Levy, F. Blin, and D. Barr (eds.), *WorldCALL: Sustainability and Computer-Assisted Language Learning*. London: Bloomsbury, 285–98.

O'Rourke, B., and Stickler, U. (2017). Synchronous Communication Technologies for Language Learning: Promise and Challenges in Research and Pedagogy. *Language Learning in Higher Education*, 7(1), 1–20. https://doi.org/10.1515/cercles-2017-0009.

Piaget, J. (1986). *Das moralische Urteil beim Kinde*. Munich: dtv Verlag.

Piccardo, E. (2010). From Communicative to Action-Oriented: New Perspectives for a New Millennium. *Contact*, 36(2), 23–35.

Pulker, H., Stickler, U., and Vialleton, E. (2021). Well-Rounded–Graduates: What Languages Can Do. In A. Plutino and E. Polisca (eds.), *Languages at Work, Competent Multilinguals and the Pedagogical Challenges of COVID-19*. Voillans: Research-Publishing Net, 23–35.

Rogers, C. R. (1983). *Freedom to Learn for the 80's*. New York: Macmillan.

Sampurna, J. (2019). *Exploring the Implementation of Online Non-Formal Project-Based Language Learning in the Indonesian Context*. PhD thesis. The Open University.

Sandhu. P., and Higgins, Ch. (2016). Identity in Post-colonial Contexts. In S. Preece (ed.), *The Routledge Handbook of Language and Identity*. London: Routledge,179–94.

Satar, H. M. (2011). Social Presence in Online Multimodal Communication: A Framework to Analyse Online Interactions between Language Learners. PhD thesis. The Open University.

Seargeant, P. (2021). *The Future of Language*. OpenLearn. Online resource. www.open.edu/openlearn/languages/the-future-language

Searle, J. R. (1969). *Speech Acts. An Essay in the Philosophy of Language*. Cambridge: Cambridge University Press.

Shen, D., Liversedge, S. P., Tian, J., et al. (2012). Eye Movements of Second Language Learners When Reading Spaced and Unspaced Chinese Text. *Journal of Experimental Psychology: Applied*, 18(2), 192–202.

Shi, L., and Stickler, U. (2018). Interaction Patterns in Synchronous Chinese Tutorials. *Innovation in Language Learning and Teaching*, 12(1), 6–23. https://doi.org/10.1080/17501229.2018.1418612

Shi, L., and Stickler, U. (2019). Using Technology to Learn to Speak Chinese. In C. Shei, M. E. M. Zikpi, and D. L. Chao (eds.), *The Routledge Handbook of Chinese Language Teaching*. London: Routledge, 509–25.

Shi, L., and Stickler, U. (2021). Eyetracking a Meeting of Minds: Teachers' and Students' Joint Attention during Synchronous Online Language Tutorials. *Journal of China Computer-Assisted Language Learning*, 1(1), 145–69.

Shi, L., Stickler, U., and Lloyd, M. E. (2017). The Interplay between Attention, Experience and Skills in Online Language Teaching. *Language Learning in Higher Education*, 7(1), 205–38.

Siemens, G. (2004). Connectivism: A Learning Theory for the Digital Age. *Elearnspace.org*. (online)

Siemens, G., and Conole, G. (2011). Connectivism: Design and Delivery of Social Networked Learning. *International Review of Research in Open and Distance Learning*, 12(3), i–iv. https://doi.org/10.1016/s0031-3203(02)00056-0

Stickler, U. (2001). Using Counselling Skills for Language Advising. In M. Mozzon-McPherson and R. Vismans (eds.), *Beyond Language Teaching towards Language Advising*. London: CILT, 40–52.

Stickler, U. (2003). Student-Centred Counselling for Tandem Learning. In T. Lewis and L. Walker, (eds.), *Autonomous Language Learning in Tandem*. Sheffield: Academy Electronic Publications, 115–22.

Stickler, U. (2004). ' … And Furthermore I Will Correct Your Mistakes': Kulturelle Unterschiede bei der Fehlerkorrektur im Tandem. *Theorie und Praxis: Österreichische Beiträge zu Deutsch als Fremdsprache*, 8, 79–93.

Stickler, U., and Emke, M. (2011). Tandem Learning in Virtual Spaces: Supporting Non-formal and Informal Learning in Adults. In Ph. Benson and H. Reinders (eds.), *Beyond the Language Classroom*. New York: Palgrave Macmillan, 146–60.

Stickler, U., and Hampel, R. (2015). Transforming Teaching: New Skills for Online Language Learning Spaces. In R. Hampel and U. Stickler (eds.), *Developing Online Language Teaching*. London: Palgrave Macmillan, 63–77.

Stickler, U., and Hampel, R. (2019). Qualitative Research In Online Language Learning: What Can It Do?. *International Journal of Computer-Assisted Language Learning and Teaching (IJCALLT)*, 9(3), 14–28.

Stickler, U., Hampel, R., Beaven, T., and Heiser, S. (2021). Supporting Language Teachers in Europe to Teach Online. REF 2021 Impact Case for Education (C23). Internal document. The Open University.

Stickler, U., Hampel, R., and Emke, M. (2020). A Developmental Framework for Online Language Teaching Skills. *Australian Journal of Applied Linguistics*, 3(1), 133–51.

Stickler, U., and Hauck, M. (eds.) (2006) Special Issue: What Does It Take to Teach Online? Towards a Pedagogy for Online Language Teaching and Learning. *CALICO Journal*, 23(3).

Stickler, U., and Shi, L. (2016). TELL us about CALL: An Introduction to the Virtual Special Issue (VSI) on the Development of Technology Enhanced and Computer Assisted Language Learning Published in the System Journal. *System*, 56, 119–26.

Stickler, U., and Shi, L. (2017). Eyetracking Methodology in SCMC: A Tool for Empowering Learning and Teaching. *ReCALL*, 29(2), 160–77.

Stickler, U., StJohn, E., and Kotschi, S. (2021). Jena CALLing. Presentation at the NALC Online Conference. The Open University, February.

Thorne, S. L. (2003). Artifacts and Cultures-of-Use in Intercultural Communication. *Language Learning & Technology*, 7(2), 38–67.

Tseng, J. J., Chai, C. S., Tan, L., and Park, M. (2020). A Critical Review of Research on Technological Pedagogical and Content Knowledge (TPACK) in Language Teaching. *Computer Assisted Language Learning*, 1-24.

Twining, P., Heller, R. S., Nussbaum, M., and Tsai, C. C. (2017). Some Guidance on Conducting and Reporting Qualitative Studies. *Computers in Education*, 106, A1–A9.

Vygotsky, L. S. (1978). *Mind in Society: The Development of Higher Psychological Processes*. Harvard: Harvard University Press.

Warschauer, M., and Healey, D. (1998). Computers and Language Learning: An Overview. *Language Teaching*, 31(2), 57–71.

Wertsch, J. V. (2002). Computer Mediation, PBL, and Dialogicality. *Distance Education*, 23(1), 105–8. https://doi.org/10.1080/01587910220124008.

Wertsch, J. V. (2007). Mediation. In H. Daniels, M. Cole, and J. V Wertsch (eds.), *The Cambridge Companion to Vygotsky*. Cambridge: Cambridge University Press, 178–92.

Whorf, B. L. (2012/1956). *Language, Thought, and Reality: Selected writings of Benjamin Lee Whorf*. Cambridge: MIT press.

Wittgenstein, L. (1974/1922). *Tractatus logico-philosophicus*. London: Routledge & Kegan Paul.

Zinger, D., Tate, T., and Warschauer, M. (2017). Learning and Teaching with Technology: Technological Pedagogy and Teacher Practice. In D. J. Clandinin and J. Husu (eds.), *The SAGE Handbook of Research on Teacher Education*. London: Sage, 577–93.

Acknowledgements

My thanks go to all the colleagues and teachers I have worked with over the years. In particular, for their help in preparing this manuscript, to Martina Emke, Lijing Shi, Regine Hampel, Annette Duensing, Teresa Pretismuir, Barbara Spicer, and Barbara Conde-Garafo, as well as to two anonymous reviewers.

Cambridge Elements ☰

Language Teaching

Heath Rose
Linacre College, University of Oxford

Heath Rose is an Associate Professor of Applied Linguistics at the University of Oxford. At Oxford, he is the course director of the MSc in Applied Linguistics for Language Teaching. Before moving into academia, Heath worked as a language teacher in Australia and Japan in both school and university contexts. He is author of numerous books, such as *Introducing Global Englishes*, *The Japanese Writing System*, *Data Collection Research Methods in Applied Linguistics*, and *Global Englishes for Language Teaching*. Heath's research interests are firmly situated within the field of second language teaching, and includes work on Global Englishes, teaching English as an international language, and English Medium Instruction.

Jim McKinley
University College London

Jim McKinley is an Associate Professor of Applied Linguistics and TESOL at UCL, Institute of Education, where he serves as Academic Head of Learning and Teaching. His major research areas are second language writing in global contexts, the internationalisation of higher education, and the relationship between teaching and research. Jim has edited or authored numerous books including the *Routledge Handbook of Research Methods in Applied Linguistics*, *Data Collection Research Methods in Applied Linguistics*, and *Doing Research in Applied Linguistics*. He is also an editor of the journal *System*. Before moving into academia, Jim taught in a range of diverse contexts including the United States, Australia, Japan, and Uganda.

Advisory Board
Brian Paltridge, *University of Sydney*
Gary Barkhuizen, ` *University of Auckland*
Marta Gonzalez-Lloret, *University of Hawaii*
Li Wei, *UCL Institute of Education*
Victoria Murphy, *University of Oxford*
Diane Pecorari, *City University of Hong Kong*
Christa Van der Walt, *Stellenbosch University*

About the Series
This Elements series aims to close the gap between researchers and practitioners by allying research with language teaching practices, in its exploration of research informed teaching, and teaching informed research. The series builds upon a rich history of pedagogical research in its exploration of new insights within the field of language teaching.

Cambridge Elements ᵉ

Language Teaching

Elements in the Series

Printed in the United States
by Baker & Taylor Publisher Services